PORTFOLIOS AND BEYOND:

Collaborative Assessment in Reading and Writing

PORTFOLIOS AND BEYOND:

Collaborative Assessment in Reading and Writing

Susan Mandel Glazer

Carol Smullen Brown

With

Phyllis DiMartino Fantauzzo

Denise Healy Nugent

Rider College

and

Lyndon W. Searfoss

Arizona State University

Christopher-Gordon Publishers, Inc.

Norwood, MA

Credit Lines:

Chapter 7: Figure 7.1 originally appeared in S.M. Glazer and L.W. Searfoss, *Reading Diagnosis and Instruction: A CALM Approach* (1988), published by Prentice-Hall. Used with permission of Allyn and Bacon.

Every effort has been made to contact copyright holders for permission to reprint borrowed material where necessary. We apologize for any oversights and would be happy to rectify them in future printings.

Christopher-Gordon Publishers, Inc.
480 Washington Street
Norwood, MA 02062

Printed in the United States of America

10 9 8 7 6 5 4   98 97 96 95 94

ISBN 0-926842-25-0

Table of Contents

Acknowledgements

In our discussions, we've agreed that our thousands of graduate and undergraduate students and the children in our classrooms must be recognized for providing us with the settings to develop our procedures. We are grateful to the classroom teachers who have helped us refine the tools we are sharing. We admire our current and former foward-looking Rider College colleagues: President J. Barton Luedeke, Walter Brower, Jerry Wayne Brown, Suzanne Gespass, William Guthrie, Jerome Megna, Carole Nicolini, Gloria Smith, Helen Stewart, Joseph Summers, and Peter Yacyk for continuously supporting all of our professional projects. We thank Andrea Bajor, Jonathan Borusovic, Jonathan Ferrante, Sadaf Hussain, Gary Nucera, Lynn Leger, Elizabeth Loik, Cori Pearson, Janine Porreca, Arne Roomann-Kurrik, Jonathan Saperstein, Kamau Suttles, Jason Yang, and their parents for permitting us to use their performance samples. Thanks to our graduate assistant Katrin-Kaja Roomann for proof-reading, typing, and organizing our final manuscript. Her professional interactions have made the process easier. We appreciate Noreen Rolle's and Margaret van Steenwyk's reviews of the text. We express appreciation to our advanced graduate students and teachers, Patricia Abitabilo, Kaye Belanger, Valerie Corcoran, Janet Freidman, Barbara A. Poole, and Deborah Russell, who helped develop the data summaries. To Sue Canavan, our publisher and supportive editor, for being as excited about our work as we are. We thank Susan L. Lytle and Lesley Mandel Morrow whose research provided us with frameworks for some of our tools. To our reviewers John Polomano, Superintendent, Audubon, New Jersey, Public Schools; Doris Roettger, Heartland Area Education Agency, Johnston,

That's when my graduate students and I began to learn more about the discrepancies between instructional practices and those used for assessment. The state mandated that formal assessment tools be used to determine students' reading abilities. The College offered a diagnostic reading course where students learned to administer and interpret formal tests. The laboratory school program was literature-based, and all language arts were integrated. Inner turmoil and confusion helped us make slow but steady modifications in our program that finally evolved into the materials in this text. We were able to develop assessment procedures that paralleled the wonderful holistic instruction that was taking place in our classrooms.

The materials we share with you have been developed collegially by teams of graduate students, faculty, and children who have attended our program since its inception in 1980. The alternative assessment procedures have changed, and are still changing to meet the needs of students and teachers.

Today's theoretical and political pressures have forced educators to look at literacy education in new ways. These pressures have driven us to share our ideas. The strategies and procedures conform with today's theories and philosophies that define current literacy learning. It is our intention to guide you, step-by-step, through our alternative assessment procedures. It is important, however, to provide a philosophical background that justifies our need to change. The background may ease the tension you may be feeling in your search for more effective assessment procedures.

S. M. G.

To A Student,

You can be proud of your strengths. You are always friendly and smiling. You get along with the children in your class and you're eager to help a friend. I really laughed when I read the story you wrote about the silly monkey.

Here are some things you might want to work on. If you read for ten minutes everyday you will read faster. When you come to a word you don't know ask someone. Sometimes you seem shy about sharing what you know with the class. I hope you will volunteer because you have great ideas!

Your teacher

"To know how to suggest is the art of teaching."

Amiel

1 An Alternative Approach To Classroom Assessment: Why Change?

We are a society that assesses constantly. We measure almost everything. We begin at birth by measuring our infants for length, weight, blood type, and other attributes. These measurements are compared to growth patterns of other infants in order to determine if our baby is near-to-normal. As children grow, their developmental patterns are compared to other children. Some of these comparisons are made based on expected behaviors described by experts who have written about child growth and development. Other comparisons result from chats with people who observe similar patterns in their own children's growth.

Assessment occurs much the same way in schools. We work with groups of students in our classrooms and assess their abilities. It is almost natural to compare performance, one student to another, especially if they are the same age. We make judgments based on our knowledge about growth and our experiences. Judgments are also made based on personal values and standards.

Often we choose to use the knowledge of experts to find out how students are growing. Expert "witnesses," as we call them, help us out of our dilemma. They have created standardized tests that are supposed to provide information about "normal expectations." These tests result in a quantitative score that illustrates each student's level of achievement. Because many people believe that these test scores "tell the truth" about performance, they have become an integral part of American education. These expert opinions have become so important that they may govern *how* children learn, *what* they learn, and even *how much* local, state, and federal funding will be available for education. Many educators and parents even choose friends. I get nervous when everyone is taking the test. I always think that I am making a mistake. I don't worry what the other kids do when I take it alone."

Test scores DO provide definitive data that add to the information about students' performance. But, there also needs to be room for the inclusion of data that attends to the humane, the sensitivities, the wonderful differences that exist in each of us.

Why Is There A Desperate Need to Consider Alternative Assessment Procedures?

We believe that there are three major reasons for the need to alter assessment procedures.

1. There has been a general discontent over literacy learning.
2. The definition of literacy education has changed.
3. Redefining literacy education has demanded changes in educational practices for teachers and learners.

Discontent Over Literacy Learning

Public discontent with education in general, and specifically the quality of literacy education, has been widespread (Farr, 1992). This concern has resulted from the standardized reading and writing test scores of our nation's school children. Poor test performance may result from differences between the test content and classroom practices. These differences have resulted from changing theories of learning, particularly literacy learning (Valencia and Pearson, 1987). The discontent has resulted in a call for the development of "a world-class education system" by the year 2000 (Campbell, 1992).

Current theoretical views of literacy that have influenced classroom practice indicate that:

- a student's prior knowledge is an important determinant of comprehension;
- appropriate reading materials have topical and structural integrity;
- inferential and critical reading are essential for constructing meaning;

- reading requires the integration and orchestration of many communication skills;
- skilled readers monitor their own comprehension using a variety of strategies for different purposes;
- good feelings about literacy activities affect success and are important goals for success in reading, writing, and oral language activities;
- good readers read fluently.

(Valencia, Pearson, Peters, Wixson, 1989)

Unfortunately, assessment in literacy, especially in reading, often contradicts these philosophical views. Assessment procedures frequently:

- fail to assess the impact of prior knowledge on comprehension by using short passages that are often isolated and unfamiliar;
- include short pieces of text that do not approximate the integrity found in most authentic texts;
- rely on materials requesting literal information;
- often test skills in isolated contexts to determine achievement for reporting purposes;
- seldom, if ever, provide vehicles for assessing students' abilities to monitor their own comprehension;
- rarely, if ever, include items that assess emotional responses to literacy activities;
- exclude vehicles for reviewing fluency in reading, writing, or oral language

(Valencia, Pearson, Peters, Wixson, 1989)

In many ways, this current period of contradictions bears similarities to times in the late 1950s when we experienced the nation's first crisis in confidence over public education in general and in the teaching of literacy with the spotlight on reading in particular (Smith, 1965). In those days, the traditional basal text for teaching reading in the elementary schools became the target of scorn. These were the very same textbooks that had come to represent the consensus among professional educators as the best way to teach reading (Chall, 1967). The concerns, then, resulted in detractors and defenders alike scrambling to amass data to support their positions.

Whole language educators also believe that these commercial materials, often prepared by less-than-adequate writers, are written to force students to practice unnecessary and fragmented reading skills in order to complete consumable workbooks (Watson, 1989).

Although harsh criticism can be disconcerting, it is one way to begin to create change. Today's educators have found ways to use the negative allegations to alter reading education. The whole language movement in reading and language arts has spread rapidly through North America. Authors, teachers, school administrators, even pediatricians use the term whole language to describe healthy, productive learning for students. It has become a fact of life.

What Has Resulted From the Whole Language Movement?

A cultishness surrounds the pioneers who spoke out in the 1980s. But it is that clustering of good people that has convinced millions that tests alone do not "tell the truth" about students' school achievement—that current theory and practice do not match. We believe that these educators have convinced communities of lay persons as well as professional educators that:

- teachers, children, and caregivers must share decisions/ control about learning;
- assessment and instruction are integrated and ongoing processes that are interdependent;
- content and skills are learned in integrated purposeful settings.

These are the elements that facilitate collegiality in classrooms. Collegial relationships foster the development of holistic programs, where assessment and instruction are ongoing collaborative activities.

Summary

Our society, although standardized test-oriented, seems ready for change. Discontentment with current systems, particularly those in literacy education, has arisen. The discontment has resulted in a new definition of literacy and changes in educational practices. These changes have led to a shift from teacher-directed classrooms to those where students and teachers share control. Assessment and instruction have become integrated, ongoing procedures. Literacy skills are learned purposefully as students engage in content area studies. It is evident to us that changes in assessment procedures are necessary to parallel the shifts in instructional processes. Students need to learn how to monitor their own growth and needs. Decisions about instruction need to be made jointly by students and their teachers. Assessment and instruction must be integrated components of all activities.

2 Assessing Classroom Environments

Lyndon W. Searfoss
Arizona State University

My contributions to this text are based on a long-time professional relationship with the authors. Their work has influenced and has been influenced by my contributions to reading/language arts. Their invitation to write this chapter provided them with an outsider's perspective of their work. It also encouraged me to rethink and rework my ideas concerning the effects of classroom environments on assessment and instruction in literacy classrooms. The authors and I agreed that my contribution had to be Chapter 2. This seemed logical since changes occur only when environments are supportive of them.

Current definitions of literacy and views of language learning have led to sweeping changes in reading and writing instruction, as discussed in Chapter 1. These changes demand the development of alternative assessment procedures. The classroom environments in which children learn, assess, and are assessed must also change. The surroundings in which children learn must be the environments where they are assessed. Classrooms must be the contexts in which the process of students' language growth is observed and assessed, with the products displayed and shared.

The classroom that promotes the interaction of assessment and instruction is a print laboratory or "print lab." It provides the physical, social, and emotional settings that allow students and teachers to read and write for real purposes, interacting and sharing language to create a community of language learners, where students' language use flourishes. (Morrow, 1989; Neuman & Roskos, 1992; Searfoss & Readence, 1989). Only when language is plentiful and rich can assessment be valid and used to guide purposeful instruction. In this chapter I will guide you to create a classroom environment that:

- encourages students to take risks while producing language;
- shares control and decision-making in language learning;
- merges instruction and assessment as a seamless web.

The Classroom Environment and Risk-taking

Classrooms that encourage risk-taking guide children to figure out not only how to read and write, but how to use reading and writing to communicate and to learn. The environment should "stretch [children's] language to the limits, to express their reactions to experiences, and to interact with each other" (Goodman, Smith, Meredith, & Goodman, 1987, p. 52). In Chapter 3 the authors ask you, as teachers, to consider these questions:

- "Do I encourage risk-taking?"
- "Can I put my values aside and accept those of students?"

These questions, and others shown in Figure 3.1, have implications for daily instruction. In Chapter 4 on assessing writing, for example, the authors caution that overemphasis on the mechanics of writing and neatness in early stages of writing development often overshadows the ideas students are trying to express. If a classroom looks too neat, we suspect that students may not be taking the risks they need to in order to develop as writers. Their natural desire to experiment with new words, new forms of writing, and new ideas may be stifled. Experimenting is messy—physically, visually, and psychologically—for children and teachers. In addition, classroom noise levels often rise in risk-taking environments. For example, while producing think-alouds students "...read a portion of text and say out loud what they are thinking as they try to make sense of it" (Chapter 5). They then continue to read more of the text, and think aloud again. This process depends upon their being able to talk out loud without concern for noise in the classroom.

In classrooms that encourage risk-taking, children make choices without first wondering if they've made the "right" choice. Students' self-selection of text, especially for think-aloud activities, sends the student the message to "take a chance, choose something to read, it is YOUR choice, and I will respect it!" When students write, their interest in revising and sharing is heightened if THEY choose the topic. We even find that students' retellings are rich in story elements when THEY have selected the text to read.

Control, Decision-making
and the Classroom Environment

Teachers, children, and caregivers must share decisions/ control about learning. (Chapter 1, p. 8)

We have discovered, over the years, that when students are involved in assessing their growth, they take control of activities. They learn what they know, and are able to discuss what they need to learn. (Chapter 4, p. 63)

My colleagues feel strongly that without shared decisions and control, classroom environments cannot encourage language growth and learning. The shift from teacher-directed environments to classrooms in which students and teachers share control (a tenet of holistic, literature-based, and integrated language arts movements) is a profound change in American classrooms. Joint decision-making by teachers and students underlies our beliefs about assessment and the assessment strategies in this book. We rely heavily on student-teacher conferences and interactions, both scheduled and spontaneous, to facilitate learning. Such settings foster interactions that help students learn how to help themselves.

In Chapter 3, for example, you meet Sarah, whose retelling productivity was beginning to get out of hand. She was surrounded by papers everywhere. When her teacher heard her beginning to talk about her dilemma—how to find and organize her ever-growing pile of papers—she "moved toward Sarah, taking the opportunity to guide the organization of the materials into four categories" (p.

practice, however, creates even more serious *validity* problems. Looking at products while ignoring the processes students use to create them provides distorted and incomplete pictures of students' abilities. These serious issues, which relate to assessment in all school subjects, continue to plague educators.

In this book, the authors constantly advocate the blending of instruction and assessment. They, like me, believe that assessment is ongoing and part of instruction. By not separating the two, we also blend process and product, two other constructs too often separated. This permits students and teachers to select samples of work while they are in process. The final product, which represents only one sample, is not valued above those samples selected for review during the process of writing.

How students arrive at the product, a piece of writing that may or may not communicate a message clearly, often tells us more about how we can guide a student than analysis of the product itself. Assessing process means we cannot act alone; we need our students involved in observing and monitoring their own products. By helping students focus on process, we guide them to discover for themselves how they can continually improve a product as they create it. Students learn how to "fix things" as they arise, rather than waiting until the teacher identifies them as "incorrect" or "unclear."

Frankly, we believe that viewing instruction and assessment as a single continuum makes assessment easier. When teachers and students wish to see progress, they can collect data from multiple sources, beginning by

- pulling a sample of something in progress;
- deciding when a product is ready for sharing;
- conferencing with a student about a work in process.

Multiple sources of data are discussed more thoroughly in Chapter 3, "Frameworks For Getting Started."

The question "How much do we collect and save?" often arises when using multiple sources. This is answered by Susan and Carol in Chapter 8, "Questions Teachers Ask." Where you store work to be saved as well as where the work originated are determined by your setting, however. My research with classroom environments

(Searfoss & Enz, 1991) suggests assessing four areas: (1) the physical organization; (2) the literacy environment; (3) how class activities are communicated with parents, administrators, and others; and (4) language use across the curriculum. These are important for creating healthy language environments for students.

We suggest that you begin the self-assessment process by sketching your classroom. Some experts in changing classroom environments begin by presenting teachers with floor plans of model classrooms to emulate. While these model plans are usually full of good suggestions, we believe self-assessment is personal. Once you create your classroom sketch, making plans for improvement follows naturally. You might want to use model floor plans as resources, and we recommend you consult them for ideas.

Several figures originally developed for research purposes (Searfoss & Enz, 1991) have been modified by the authors for this text. Figure 2.1 can guide you to assess the literacy environment. We recommend that the environment in your classroom be tailored to the age and grade levels of your students. Modify these forms to fit your needs by adding or deleting items.

It is important to communicate with parents, administrators, and others involved in students' learning in school. We've used Figure 2.2 to document how class activities are communicated to these people.

FIGURE 2.1

LITERACY ENVIRONMENT

Organization encourages language production: Reading, Writing, Listening, Oral language

Centers/Areas (tailored to age, grade level)

	Check	Comments:
Library		
Home center		
Dramatic play		
Day-to-day		
Print production		
Listening		
Others		
Materails		
Tradebooks		
Magazines		
Reference books		
Others		
Literacy Display		
Walls		
Bulletin boards		
Others		

FIGURE 2.2

COMMUNICATION WITH THE PUBLIC

Communication: Class activities are communicated to parents, administrators, and colleagues. Purposes of these activities is related through:

	Check	Comments:
Regular newsletters (weekly, monthly)		
Regular notes/comments of student progress		
Regular overviews of class activities		
Invitations to parents to participate		
Participation in local whole-language support groups		
Other (list)		

Copyright © 1991 by L. Searfoss and B. Enz. Used by permission of the authors.

Since language skills are the vehicle for communicating across the entire school curriculum, we strongly recommend that you take notice of the language activities in content areas. Figure 2.3, used regularly, can guide you to alter your program appropriately.

FIGURE 2.3

LANGUAGE ACROSS THE CURRICULUM

	READING	WRITING	ORAL LANGUAGE (Speaking/Listening)
WHOLE GROUP			
SMALL GROUP			
PAIRED			
INDIVIDUAL			

Put a mark in each box when students are engaged in an activity that fits, e.g. small group listening or paired reading. OR, write in the content area, (e.g. SCI, SS, READ, MATH). AFTER completing your usual weekly activities, go back and fill in boxes as a double check to note where you are concentrating language across curriculum. Empty boxes are not "wrong." If week after week, no checks appear in a box or no activities are marked SS or SCI, then you need to revise activities to "get language going" in different settings and content areas.

Copyright © 1991 by L. Searfoss and B. Enz. Used by permission of the authors.

Self-monitoring guides for developing an environment rich in literacy activities serve as change agents. They guide teachers to see their classrooms in a new light. An awareness of what exists can also lead to an awareness of what is needed to improve the quality of the environment. My colleagues and I have used Figure 2.4, another form of classroom self-assessment, to guide the physical organization and use of supplies, equipment and other resources necessary for a print-rich environment.

FIGURE 2.4

ASSESSING THE LITERACY ENVIRONMENT

Three general questions guide our observations of the classroom environment:
- Does the arrangement of equipment encourage language production?
- Does the environment encourage independent reading and writing?
- Are reading materials, texts, and references part of the learning environment?

Yes	No		
____	____	1.	Are tables and chairs arranged for individual work?
____	____	2.	Can chairs and tables be arranged for group work?
____	____	3.	Are permanent areas housing equipment in constant use, appropriately managed for student access?
____	____	4.	Are trade books in a central location?
____	____	5.	Is there a lounge area (library-type) for reading?
____	____	6.	Is there an area for typewriters and computers?
____	____	7.	Is there an area for acting?
____	____	8.	Is there large chalkboard space for individual and group writing?
____	____	9.	Are there large sheets of paper on walls for composing?
____	____	10.	Is there an area to listen to tapes and recordings?
____	____	11.	Are a variety of writing tools and materials available?

- pencils/crayons
- paints
- erasers
- typewriters
- ballpoint/ink pens
- chalk
- colored markers

Have Students Take Responsibility for Planning Their Daily Activities

Beginning each day by reviewing their responsibilities is one way to start. Students can routinely write lists in a log or journal the first few minutes of the school day. Very young children might want to dictate them to the teacher, or a parent volunteer. We suggest that students review their daily accomplishments at the end of each school day. These can be written or discussed orally, either individually or with the teacher. Looking these over, and then making a list for "today," which includes tasks not completed the day before, reinforces goals to accomplish. When a student appears to be drifting, not working at a task, or interfering with other learners, you might ask "Which of your goals for today are you working on?" or "Show me which goal(s) you have completed so far." As students become more and more adept at self-monitoring, they will need you less and less. This provides you with time to guide those students who appear to be unable to take charge.

Use the Classroom Environment to its Fullest

Figure 2.3, "Language Across the Curriculum," (p. 19) is a quick way to assess how effectively you have planned for a variety of groupings (whole, small, paired, and individual). It is important to monitor whether you are including activities across the curriculum in each block (e.g. small group writing as part of a social studies activity). This will give you a picture of classroom life from students' perspectives. If some blocks have no entries week after week, then you may need to revise your planning and introduce more variety in using language across the curriculum.

Cooperative learning groups, when group tasks are meaningful, encourage independence and language growth. As defined by Whisler and Williams (1991), cooperative learning "...is a teaching strategy that enables students to work collaboratively together in structured heterogeneous groups toward a common goal while being held individually accountable" (p. 6). Some groups form because of common interests, others may be assigned by students or teachers, and still others are created spontaneously, disbanding when the need for collaboration no longer exists.

Once your environment has taken shape, be certain you do not discourage the natural flow of activity in the classroom. Set guidelines with your students for how many learners can use an area at one time and get their suggestions for monitoring and enforcing classroom rules. With students working independently in pairs, alone, and in small groups, your environment will be used to its fullest.

Summary

The classroom is the setting for the assessment procedures advocated in this book. Make certain that your classroom environments encourage risk-taking, shared control, and the seamless webbing of instruction with assessment. When these elements are natural in your classroom, you have created a rich environment in which to assess students' language learning.

3 Frameworks for Getting Started

The process of change can be startling, uncomfortable, and stressful. Why do it? When the cognitive and emotional development of our nation's children is at stake, there is no choice. If you decide to take the first step and begin to think seriously about changing classroom assessment procedures, you must expect to feel "out of control" at times. At other times you may be ready to give up (but don't). Getting started, although difficult, can be an exciting experience. This chapter is your guide for beginning.

Creating Alternative Assessment Procedures in Classrooms: How To Begin

Although prescription is contrary to our beliefs, here we are prescribing five steps toward change. The "prescription" is meant to guide you to develop unique descriptions of literacy development for each student you teach.

Step One

Begin by creating an environment conducive to collaborative assessment. You need to think about making your environment risk-free. We always ask ourselves how we would feel if we were in our students' shoes. If we like the feelings, we continue. If not, we change activities, environments, and situations until comfort is achieved. The questions in Figure 3.1 can serve as guidelines for creating such an environment.

FIGURE 3.1

Do I Encourage Risk-taking?	Example
Can I put my values aside and accept those of my student?	A messy desk may be difficult for you to work on, but comfortable for a student.
Do I praise specifically so students know what is the desired behavior?	"I like the way you decided that you needed help editing your paper. You're able to assess your own needs!"
Am I able to parallel students' ideas or reactions when I respond?	Student: "I hate this work!" Teacher: "Sometimes I hate my work, too. But I plow through it because if feels good when I'm done!"

It may be difficult to accept the values of students. It is difficult, also, to "let go" and give control to children. To guide students to assess their own growth, they need to feel the power. They need to know that they can voice their feelings, opinions, and ideas. Children need to be in an environment that gives them license to express themselves. Activities that say, "It's okay to tell what you think" can be carried out in large and small groups and in individual discussions. The following activities should serve as guides for developing these for your students.

Large or Whole Class Activity

Encourage your students to talk about a current event. Begin by discussing the event yourself. Use phrases like "I feel....," "In my opinion...." We have found that when discussing controversial events such as students' parents divorcing or drug use, students will voice ideas. The key to success is LISTENING. Listen to your students and accept what each one says, without making judgments. You will find that other students will react to peer contributions. You will also discover that your students will learn, intuitively, that they have the freedom to comment. Lack of criticism or judgment on your part provides them with that information.

Talks with special teachers	Getting advice for altering instruction to meet needs.	When I need to.	That's why I do it; to make instruction effective.
Take notes while children work	Put all of the data I can about a child together to solve the puzzle about learning.	All the time—in class, at break, at home.	I write about children's behaviors as they work. So, it does match instruction.

In addition to reviewing testing materials with colleagues, think about your goals for students and changes in your classroom, as well. Figure out ways to move from your more formal structures for assessing growth to our collaborative approaches. You will find learning logs, suggested in Step One above, helpful for moving from teacher-to student-directed assessment. Your learning logs and your students' logs add information that supports change.

We recall one child who asked Valerie to read his story. After he read it, the student asked, "Do you like it?" Valerie's response was, "I like it if you do." The student responded, "No, I don't like it." "Well," responded Valerie, you can do one of three things. You can throw it away and write another, reread it and fix it up, or share it with your partner to get his opinion." The child said, "O.K." His facial expressions showed that this was probably the first time he was asked to make some judgments about his own work. "I guess I'll throw it away and start again," was his response. His agreeable teacher smiled, and accepted his decision. As the child walked toward the waste basket, he stopped, turned back to Valerie and said, "I like it a little." The smiling teacher was all the child needed in order to encourage him to say, "I'm going to fix it up."

Step Three.

Once current procedures have been reviewed with colleagues— other teachers, the reading/language arts specialist, and school administrators—a task force could address the following issues:

- What do we want to keep? Why?
- What do we want to eliminate? Why?
- What do we need to add to our assessment program? Why?

Answers to these questions can come from activities in Chapter 2, and the rest of the text. Begin, one step at a time. Start small. Set one afternoon aside each week to carry out a collaborative assessment activity. You might decide to begin with a small number of students. If you have large classes, and limited time, engage in the assessment activities that are compatible with these restrictions. You must make some decisions, however, about commitment to change. In order to make assessment ongoing, you may have to find ways to convince administrators, fellow teachers, and parents that class schedules might need alteration. Moving from restricted 45-minute periods, for example, to two hour time blocks is an important beginning.

Step Four

Discussions among professionals after reviewing current trends and goals might result in the following conclusions:

- that a match between procedures used for assessment and those for instruction is necessary;
- that children need to be part of the assessment process;
- that some new procedures are necessary, and some older ones can be retained.

Such conclusions provide the basis for developing a series of needs. Next, review your needs and develop charts such as the one shown in Figure 3.3, which can guide you to alter your programs.

You may also need additional materials, furniture, storage bins, and even parent volunteers to get started. Books, science and social studies materials, art supplies, and props for dramatizing the

content of stories will help you grow. The more materials there are
to enhance learning, the more choices students will be able to make
on their own.

FIGURE 3.3

We Believe We Need	Why?
We need information, in addition to the required tests, to find out abilities in reading comprehension, writing, and other language arts skills areas.	Any test tells about the child's ability to perform on THAT test. It does not replicate what we do in school. We need to use a procedure that resembles what children do when they read and write in school.
We need to find ways to guide children to understand why tests are important. They also need to know that tests are only one way to find out something about what they know.	It is important that children feel responsibile for their learning. They MUST, therefore, learn as much about their performances as possible.
We need to find ways to guide children to observe their performance. We want them to be able to note their strengths (what they know), and needs (what each needs to learn).	Taking responsibility is encouraged with concrete information. If children know about their abilities, they will be encouraged to take responsibility for improving those abilities.
We need to involve parents as part of the change process.	We need their support. Involvement encourages support, which is beneficial to their children.
We need to have children involved.	Children will benefit from many of these great suggestions.

Sufficient storage space is important for creating independent learners. Students need "THEIR" space to collect and store materials. The ownership of such space places a special value on work samples. Although space may be a restriction, use whatever you can find.

One of our teachers created a wall unit from cardboard cartons. The students piled one on top of the other. One of our teachers referred to this cardboard furniture as oversized safe deposit boxes. This phrase described the value for the contents of each.

Step Five

Gather student work samples. Encourage students to gather their own. Samples of students' work are the data that provide information that drives instruction. Multiple data from all sorts of activities help to tell stories about students' growth. We collect data by taking notes about students during activities, teaching children to review and write about their products (self-assessments), collecting photographs and videos of students in action, reviewing writing samples, retellings in response to reading, and oral think-alouds about reading. These procedures are our windows for learning about students.

Teacher Notes and Narratives about Students

Pat wrote the following on a piece of paper while watching Kevin write a story:

Setting: Kevin, by himself, writing a story. Took unlined paper. Began to write. Crumpled paper. Took lined paper. Began to write. Erased. Wrote and erased again. Crumpled paper, took it to waste basket. Took unlined paper. Knelt on knees, bit lip. Began writing. Wrote for seven minutes. Looked up. Looked back to paper, and appeared to read it. Put paper in front of Peter, "See my story!" Pulls away immediately.

These objective notes describe Kevin's behavior. Pat wrote WHAT she saw, not her interpretations of the behaviors. In this instance, she used Post-It Notes. Other teachers may use notebook paper.

We have created a progress report sheet for our teachers. Summary of strengths are recorded in the first column; needs, usually in the form of questions, go in the center one; and finally, instructional guidelines based on strengths and needs are listed in the third column. Figure 3.4 (on page 36) is used throughout this text. This sheet provides us with a vehicle for reporting weekly summaries of achievement, and serves as a vehicle for planning.

Students' Self-assessments

Figure 3.5 (on page 37) was written by Andrea Bajor after a day in school.

Photographs and Video Recordings

A picture of activity, moving or still, provides materials for continuous review. Looking, again and again, at the same pictures of behavior permits thoughtful insights and interpretations of data.

Writing Samples

Compositions, letters, reports, drawings, retellings after reading, and other materials written by hand, dictated to a peer or adult, orally recorded and transcribed, or composed on a computer are major sources of material for assessment. A variety of writing samples over time is essential for assessment purposes. It is important that children include handwritten samples of their writing as often as possible. Handwritten materials provide information about writing abilities, and also:

- small muscle coordination
- evidence of learning disabilities that might be related to visual perceptual deficits and organizational disfunctions
- behaviors related to syndromes associated with dysgraphia (inability to use the coding system to write) and dyslexia (the inability to use the coding system to read).

FIGURE 3.4

PROGRESS REPORT

Student's Name_____ Teacher's Name_____

Time period: From:_____   To:_____

AREA: (check one) Comprehension_____   Composition_____   Vocabulary_____
          Independence/Self-Esteem_____   Self-Monitoring_____

STRENGTHS	NEEDS (Questions)	PLANS

FIGURE 3.5

Name: Andrea Bair	Things I can Do	Things I'm Working On	Things I Want to Learn
Writing	I can write long & detailed stories.	I am working on making longer/shorter introductions	I want to learn to write shorter stories instead of long ones.
Vocabulary Building	make new words for my writing	thinking of new words	I want to learn definitions of big numongous weird words.
Reading	I can read big, long, fat books	I'm Reading Down a dark Hall	I want to learn how to finish a book when I start it.

Students' writing samples, when created in responses to reading, provide information about comprehension as well as composition. The data, and the storage space are the most important things for getting started with this step. They are visible changes that inform students and visitors to your classroom that something different is happening.

Retellings in Response to Reading

Some students demonstrate comprehension after reading best by retelling, orally, what they remember. Retellings, recorded on tape and transcribed, become the data for assessment.

Oral Think-alouds about Reading

We guide our student to learn how to think out loud about what they read. We ask them to read a sentence, and at times longer sections of text. Then we ask them to say aloud what they are thinking as they make sense of the text. Reviewing this data helps students to consider multiple ways of thinking about the text.

How to Continue

Once you've begun to make small changes, things will be easier. You will begin to ask yourself many questions. The first question asked by most of our teachers is, "How much data should we save?" We find that we—teachers and students—collect everything: drawings, stories, research projects, all kinds of reading and writing.

Some students like to save EVERYTHING. Others do not. If your students and you were to save everything, the volume of material might be overwhelming. You need to decide together with your students which data best represents accomplishments, and which provides the best information for planning instruction. Weekly discussions with children provide the vehicles for making these decisions.

Many of our children, especially those in the elementary grades, like to take work samples home to show their parents. This has been a problem for us at times. We have solved the problem in several ways:

- the child and teacher decide together what can go home;
- a decision is made concerning how long the sample can stay home or if it is to be returned to the data base;
- photocopies are sometimes made;
- diaries that include personal communications between a student and her teacher do not go home. The privacy to chat in written form, confidentially, must be respected.

Student immersion in the assessment process ought to begin immediately. Once they're involved, we use the above guidelines for continuing self-assessment activities that result in independent, self-monitoring learners.

Involving Students

We have found that the best way to begin the collaborative assessment process with children is to talk about the process. Children need to know what is happening and why. Begin by doing what children do naturally. Show them how to be collectors of their own data. Select a container—a folder, basket, bucket, shoe box, part of a file drawer—for collecting data. These containers, kept in a central location in the classroom, encourage children to regularly review their productions.

Begin by talking to students about their samples. Encourage them to do as much of the talking as possible. Guides included in this text help them notice characteristics about their products. Talking about products will lead to writing descriptions about what they know and what they need to learn. Students, with time and practice, will jot notes to themselves about products.

Our experiences have led us to believe that it is best to guide children to assess growth from the very first moment they enter the room. The following dialogue is a transcript of one child's first five minutes in his new classroom setting.

Teacher: Hi, Jon.

Jon: Hi, Ms. Abitabilo. Where do I go?

Teacher: You can take any table you like. (As the child begins to move about selecting his space, the teacher hands him a basket.) Here is a basket with your name on it. Everything you do can go in here. I would like you to save everything you do. Then we can look at it regularly.

Jon: Everything? Even the junky stuff?

Teacher: Everything. And, you know what, I don't think anything you do will be junky, even if it's the first draft of a story. (Ms. Abitabilo gets some stationery, and begins to write a letter.) I'm writing letters to all of my new students. I didn't have time to finish them last night. There is a list of names of the children in our class. You might want to write a letter to one of your friends. There is a mail envelope for each.

Jon: O.K. (The child gets a piece of stationery, and begins to write for several minutes. He crumples the paper, and throws it away. He begins again, and again, throws the second paper away. Jon begins a third time, and starts to crumple that piece of paper too.)

Teacher: You might want to save your drafts.
Jon: What's a draft?
Teacher: The papers you are throwing away.
Jon: Oh I didn't like them so I threw them away, and
          started again.
Teacher: That's great. Tell me why you didn't like them.
Jon: (Shrugging his shoulders) Um, I'm not sure.
Teacher: That's great. It is good to know that you can tell
          that you are not sure why you didn't like them.
          If you keep them in your basket, you could look
          at them later, and you might decide what you
          did that made you want to throw them away.
          That's what I do.
Jon: No.
Teacher: Well, I'm going to ask you to save everything
          you write, so that you and I can review them—
          look them over again and again.
Jon: Why?
Teacher: Why do you think?
Jon: I don't know.
Teacher: Well, what do you think?
Jon: So I can do better?
Teacher: That's one good reason. And if you look them
          over you can decide what it is that you would
          like to do better. (Jon goes to the waste basket,
          uncrumples one of the drafts, and puts it into
          the basket.) That's a good idea. You already
          have one piece of data to look at.

Conferences can be scheduled or they can also occur spontaneously, as did the one above, because the need arises. Once children
know the process, they collect everything. Our children hoard their
data. Some may view the process competitively, and things can get
out of hand. "I've got more in my basket than you do," is a common
phrase heard at the beginning of the year. These comments disap-
pear, however, once children learn how to look at their samples.
After collecting three weeks of drafts, one eleven-year-old had
already realized the purposes for collecting his stories, drawings,

Throughout this book we include various strategies for guiding students to become independent readers and writers. We also include sheets that we use to guide us in assessing student work samples. Just saving work isn't enough. We have found that we need to select samples that stand out in some way. These outstanding samples help us come to some conclusions about growth and needs. We also need vehicles for helping us summarize and report progress periodically. We are sharing, in this text, the various summary and reporting vehicles we use to review our students' development and to guide our planning of instructional activities. We also need to spontaneously find strategies for guiding each student to use the environment in order to learn to read and write effectively.

Summary: Where Do We Go from Here?

Taking the first step is most difficult. Now that you've begun, forge ahead. The slow and tedious process will emerge, over time, facilitated by collegial, risk-taking actions mentioned here.

The rest of the text is organized much like Sarah's portfolio. Each chapter explains processes for collecting, organizing, and summarizing data with students. The most unique materials are "dual" tools: those for teachers and those for students that facilitate parallel/collegial review. These parallel forms result in summaries of growth and needs that share the same language. One is usually written by the teacher and another by the student and others interested in reviewing growth using the student's point of view. Our procedures are illustrated with samples collected by several children throughout a school year. Our assessment and instructional activities deomonstrate the over time nature of holistic reviews. The data summaries illustrate the importance of generic tools that can be used for all grades and curriculum areas.

4 Assessing Writing

Do We Agree on What Writing Is?

Writing is a developmental process that evolves much like oral language. Many studies have demonstrated that growth in written language parallels oral language development (Clark & Clark, 1977; Clay, 1975, 1991; Halliday, 1975; Harste, Burke & Woodward, 1982; Loban, 1963; Olson, 1977; Ruddell & Haggard, 1985). Both writing and speaking develop through functional opportunities, practice, and modeling by others. The process can be likened to the stages of development outlined by Piaget and Vygotsky. Vygotsky writes "...as the child gains proficiency, task demands are raised until the child is functioning independently and the teacher functions as a supportive observer" (1962, p. 101). No amount of direct instruction can hasten the process, but environment, social interactions, modeling, and instruction facilitate growth.

Over the years, both instruction and assessment of writing have focused on mechanics: spelling, punctuation, capitalization, segmentation, and neatness. The appearance of the text has often seemed to be more important than its content. Teachers' comments and the focus on mechanics have often minimized the production of ideas (Petty & Finn, 1981). As a result, these overshadowed ideas have suffered from the overemphasis on the mechanics of writing. Marked-up papers and comments frequently have conveyed little meaning to the writer (Butler, 1980; Hahn, 1981; Sommers, 1982; Sperling and Freedman, 1987).

Because of discrepancies over definitions of writing, assessment of writing in classrooms has often been a source of consternation for teachers (Searle and Dillon, 1980). When the assessment process goes beyond sentence construction and mechanics, and when elements such as ideas, organization, tone, and audience awareness are assessed, teachers often become anxious. This occurs because of the subjective nature of assessing writing. Subjectivity in assessing these areas is natural, since each teacher brings different expectations and experiences to the process, and since developmental guidelines in these areas are not established.

In recent years, the focus in classrooms has begun to reflect the notion that writing, much like oral language, is developmental. Teachers now are focusing attention on ideas. Mechanics, once the important aspect, are left until the end of the writing, when children refine their work in preparation to share with an audience. In schools throughout our nation the process—writing and rewriting text and discussing these activities—has taken precedence over final product, the writing project itself. Instruction has focused on guiding processes, sometimes at the expense of the products themselves. This causes much confusion for assessment purposes. Teachers, students, and their parents often ask, "What is important, the working habits that students use to create a product, or the product itself?"

We have learned as we work with children that process IS important. But, products—children's stories, poems, letters, messages to each other, as well as notes—are as important as the processes used to create them. We believe that both the processes and the products of composing are important. Both guide us to see strengths and needs as our students move through stages of writing development. Therefore, we assess the processes our students use as they write as well as the products they create.

Writing is a Developmental Process

Children move through writing stages developmentally, over time. Each child develops differently. Figures 4.1 and 4.2 dramatically demonstrate the varieties of strengths and needs that exist among children who are the same age. These autobiographies were both written by second grade girls.

FIGURE 4.1

Sadaf

I am the only child. I'm good at telling jokes and riddles. I'm a muslim. I love to play and work. Everyone is my friend. My bike is big. My house is green. My favorte fuit is mango. I love to write. I go to chuch. I am the best kid in the class. My fuvate shows are dangoros women, Famliy fun Bart simpson. I love to write in aribic. I like mazes and to conet the dots. I will make the kabka with Nabila. I am seven. I can write neater than this. I won Nick toon shuts. I am an ant to more than twelve children My hair is black. I go to lanning school. I read very well.

FIGURE 4.2

Erin

MY PAt
I have to dogs Moly and Maks. wuoṇs a gerl and wuoṇs a boy. the boy is wout and the gerl is blak. the gerl digs.

Translation of Figure 4.2:
I have two dogs Molly and Macks. One's a girl and one's a boy. The boy is white and the girl is black. The girl digs.

At first inspection, it appears that Sadaf is in transition to the emergent writing stage while Erin is entering the beginning writing stage. Upon closer inspection, however, it is clear these two writers are both in the beginning writing stage, exhibiting different strengths and needs. Sadaf is a prolific writer who uses mostly correct spellings, capitalization, and punctuation. However, she usually uses the same sentence pattern construction, beginning sentences with "I" or "My." She also does not maintain a clear focus throughout, instead writing a string of unrelated sentences about herself.

Erin uses a great deal of invented spelling based on the phonemic sound of the word, little capitalization, and has written briefly. However, she gives a title to her selection, uses various sentence beginnings, as well as compound sentence construction, and evidences a sense of story throughout.

Differences in children's writing exist because children grow at their own pace and pattern of development. These differences can be described through a series of stages (Clay, 1975; Glazer & Searfoss, 1988). Clay (1975) has defined a series of principles that illustrate preschool children's emergence into writing. Dr. Clay, one of the first to guide professionals to begin to look at children's scribbles as writing, discusses writing development through the kindergarten years. Graves (1983), Calkins (1986), and Routman (1988) are among the teachers who have provided further information about writing development. These reflective practitioners discuss the processes through which children move in order to learn to communicate in written form. Their works have permitted us to extend descriptions of writing development to elementary school-aged students.

Assessing Writing

Children's writing, like all writing, illustrates their knowledge about written language. The things they need to know about writing are included in the Writing Assessment Summary sheet (Figure 4.7), our tool for summarizing and describing elements of students' writing (p. 57). After asking questions about a student's work samples, we categorize the answers (data) into four areas: writing stage, sentence construction, mechanics, and audience awareness.

For example, when reviewing the student's audience awareness we might ask, "Is the child able to express his or her ideas in writing so that an audience of peers (or adults) can understand the content? Is the writing organized?" Asking about the student's ability to structure sentences could begin by asking, "How many different sentence patterns does the child use? What syntactic elements make the text interesting to read?" We assess each of these four areas by asking questions about the aspects of the writing listed on this sheet (see Figures 4.7 and 4.8). We use the Writing Stage Assessment Sheet, Figure 4.4, Page 53 (Glazer & Searfoss, 1988) for identifying a student's developmental writing stage. Knowing this is critical for determining the kinds of instructional procedures needed.

The first thing we assess is the student's stage of writing development. Since these stages remain relatively constant for periods of time, one sheet may be used for an entire reporting period. We begin by identifying the strengths exhibited. Then we determine whether the needs that seem to be present are truly needs or whether the behaviors are developmentally appropriate for that stage of writing development.

For example, Figure 4.3 was written by Daniela, a kindergarten girl. We can see that Daniela is in transition from the prewriting stage to the beginning writing stage. Strengths in her writing include writing a complete thought on paper, an awareness of sound-symbol relationships, and a consistent use of consonant combinations to represent words. She is also accurate in her letter formation.

FIGURE 4.3

Translation: Last Summer I went on a roller coaster - Last spring I went to my house

Daniela's immediate needs include recognizing that words have spaces between them when written in phrases and sentences and distinguishing between upper and lower case letters. Daniela is not developmentally ready to focus on appropriate punctuation. These skills will develop over time as she writes in functional settings. We use Figure 4.4 to assess writing stages. This one is completed for Daniela.

We believe it is important to note what a student is developmentally ready to learn. When a student is in the beginning writing stage, for example, he or she generally uses the same sentence patterns again and again. Direct instruction cannot change this developmental trend. One beginning writer wrote, "I like milk" and "I like Nintendo." Instructing children at this stage, therefore, to use a sentence starter such as "Today ..." results, at best, in the starter attached to the original pattern. This is illustrated when this same seven-year-old wrote, "Today I like candy," and "Today I like Nintendo."

Conversely, a student who has moved into the emergent writing stage presents ideas which are well focused, and uses a variety of sentence patterns. Another seven-year-old, for example, who was assessed as an emergent writer wrote,

> Today on my way to grandma's I fell. I hurt my knee. It was bleeding and I got my new jeans dirty. I am scared my Mom will get mad.

This student, because she has moved into the next developmental stage, will not revert back to writing sentences like, "Today I am going to my grandma's. Today I fell. Today I was bleeding. Today I tore my new jeans."

FIGURE 4.4

STAGES OF WRITING DEVELOPMENT

Child's Name: Daniela   Age: 6 (June)

BEHAVIOR	COMMENTS

STAGE 1: PREWRITING

Scribbles without preconception . . . . ._____
Shows interest in words and letters. . . . . . ._____
Preplans writing and drawing projects . . . ._____
Spends long periods on these projects . . ._____
Shows space relationships and
   critiques own work. . . . . ._____
Recognizes and names letters. . . . . ._____
Writing of words lacks sound/symbol
   relationship . . . . ._____

(STAGE 2: THE BEGINNING WRITER)

Labels drawings. ._____
Makes lists of same-pattern sentences. . . ✓ (Last summer I/Last spring I)
Develops a sense of story . . . . ._____
Includes personal experiences in writing . ✓_____
Overuses structures . . . . ✓
Invents spelling . . . . ✓ (smr-summer, 1st-last)
Requests help with spelling. . . . . .____not yet_____
Uses some punctuation. . . . . .____none_____

STAGE 3: THE EMERGENT WRITER

Writes with purpose. . . . . ._____
Can focus thoughts through writing. . . . . ._____
Uses varied sentence structures. . . . . . . ._____
Spells using mostly conventional patterns_____
Uses correct punctuation. . . . . ._____

Summary
Statement: Writes about personal experiences; uses
complete sentences; single, pairs, combined consonants
                                    correspond to phonemes.
Stage: Beginning stage

A student will, however, exhibit behaviors from several stages at the same time while in transition from one stage to another. Specific instructional guidance at that time is often helpful in facilitating his or her moving into that next stage. Students will progress naturally through stages only when they have many opportunities to observe others (such as teachers and peers) writing and to write regularly themselves.

As mentioned several times, children of the same age and in the same grade will exhibit a variety of competencies within the same writing stage. Variations depend upon children's experiences with ideas. When children who are in the beginning writing stage write about familiar ideas, or write in familiar genres, their compositions might include characteristics typical of emergent writers. When topics or formats, such as a research report, are unfamiliar, these same youngsters tend to write as if they were at an earlier stage of development.

It is interesting to notice and then record the varied abilities of children of the same age. These differences continue to exist in writing throughout all ages. The writing shown in Figures 4.5 and 4.6, written by Michael and Jeffrey, demonstrate such differences. Both students were entering eighth grade, and were fourteen years of age when they wrote these samples. Both pieces of writing are assessed using a Writing Assessment Summary sheet, shown in Figures 4.7 and 4.8. Both students seem to be emergent writers. Yet their texts are quite different in levels of audience awareness, as the Summary sheets demonstrate.

Both boys' writing illustrates a pattern typical of their age; their writing consists of one continuous paragraph. An instructional mini-lesson might focus on paragraph construction. Their individual needs would be recognized and addressed through a flip-flop of instruction, self-monitoring, teacher monitoring, and modeling.

We find that the stage of writing often seems dependent upon the kind of writing in which the student is engaged. Our students typically exhibit similar proficiencies when producing similar kinds of discourse. Narrative seems most natural for them. They usually create more ideas and use more varied sentence patterns in this form then they do when they write other forms. Knowledge about story structures is usually acquired before school age (Stein & Glenn, 1979), whereas we have found that the structural elements of other genres often require more formal training. In our observations of children's writing during the past ten years, we have found that narrative discourse seems easier to comprehend and remember than other genres (definition, description, exposition, and persuasion).

FIGURE 4.5

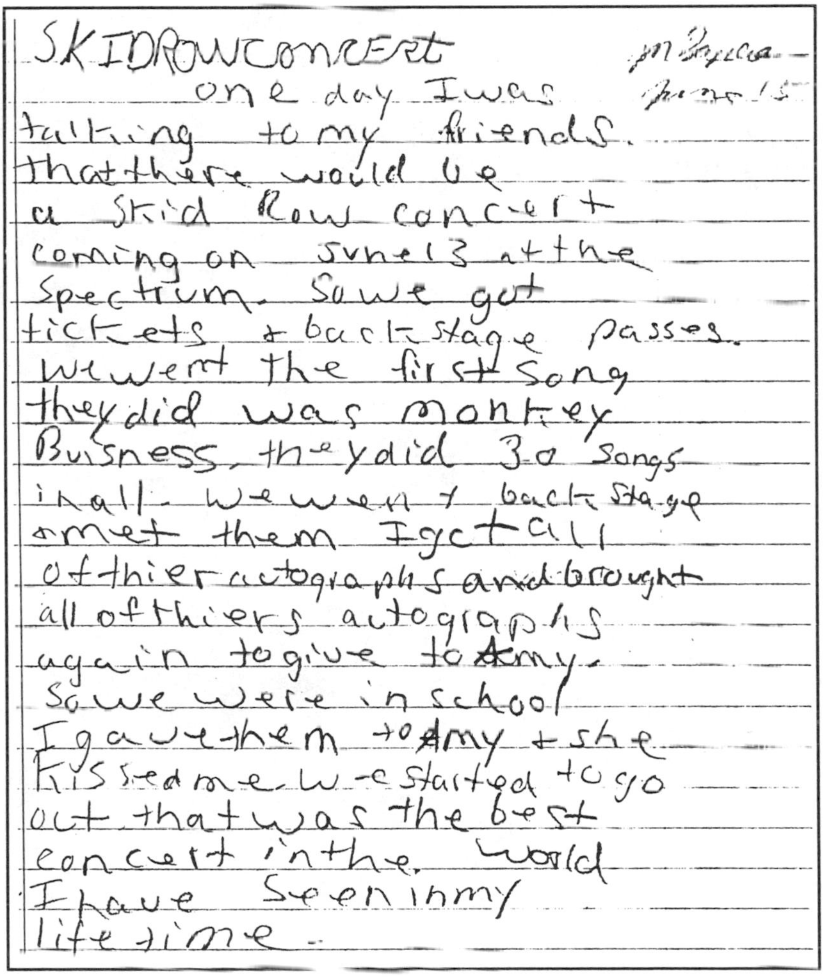

SKIDROWCONCERT

one day I was talking to my friends. that there would be a Skid Row concert coming on June 13 at the Spectrum. So we got tickets + backstage passes. we went the first Song they did was monkey Buisness, they did 30 Songs in all. we went backstage omet them I get all of thier autographs and brought all of thiers autographs again to give to Amy. So we were in school I gave them to Amy + she Kissed me we started to go out that was the best concert in the world I have seen in my life time ..

FIGURE 4.6

I'm going to tell this reader (Which means you) that this will be about how I feel about pollution and the way its effecting our world today. I'm sad now these days that when the first window on the bus is opened I smell polluted air. I'm sad to hear about acid rain or hear someone bring back memories on the huge oil spill that Sadam Husain caused during the gulf war. It ashame to see headlines on newspapers about animal dying because of plastic beer or soda holders or from plastic in the ocean. Our world is changing; just like its been since God created it. But now its changing for the worse. If we don't do something about people cutting down rain forests or factories polluting the air... Well... I think you've already heard what's going to happen. Please recycle. What makes it even worse is that Newtown can't recycle because township leaders don't want to. They feel its too much of a bother. It makes me feel important that I can do something in the world when I'm able to recycle. So please save our world.

FIGURE 4.7

WRITING ASSESSMENT SUMMARY

Child's Name: __Michael__   Age: __14__

	Comments
WRITING STAGE	
Prewriting - (Scribbles, recognizes names and letters, spelling is prephonemic)	
Beginning - (Labels, requests help, repeats sentence patterns, invents spelling)	
Emergent - (purposeful in writing, <u>focuses</u> thoughts, varies content, <u>spelling is conventional</u>)	maintains theme throughout
SENTENCE CONSTRUCTION	
Writes one word sentences	
Repeats sentence patterns	
Varies sentence structure	yes
Uses other elements of syntax for creating interesting text	no
MECHANICS	
Handwriting is legible	yes, spacing crowded, letter formation awkward
Uses punctuation: (periods, commas, other)	some periods - not consistent
Uses capitalization	yes, sentence beginnings, proper names
Spelling development trends	mostly correct/needs their/there rule
AUDIENCE AWARENESS	
Language addresses intended audience	sporadically
Focuses on topic	part - switches theme halfway through
Uses varied vocabulary	no - mostly basic words
Organizes text logically	somewhat - "jumps" in time confusing.
Relates sentences to each other	somewhat - (a few unrelated appear).
Writes in logical sequence	yes, but ending not clear
Aware of genre conventions (narrative, descriptive, explanatory, persuasive)	yes

Instructional Needs

immediate need - use of consistent punctuation to separate ideas; paragraphs to help clarify ideas. spelling lesson - their/there rule

FIGURE 4.8

WRITING ASSESSMENT SUMMARY

Child's Name: __Jeffrey__   Age: __14__

	Comments
WRITING STAGE	
Prewriting - (Scribbles, recognizes names and letters, spelling is prephonemic)	
Beginning - (Labels, requests help, repeats sentence patterns, invents spelling)	
Emergent - (purposeful in writing, focuses thoughts, varies content, spelling is conventional)	maintains definite focus
SENTENCE CONSTRUCTION	
Writes one word sentences	
Repeats sentence patterns	
Varies sentence structure	✓ uses clauses, various sentence patterns
Uses other elements of syntax for creating interesting text	- creates questions for audience ✓ - on-going dialogue with audience
MECHANICS	
Handwriting is legible	✓
Uses punctuation: (periods, commas) other)	✓
Uses capitalization	✓
Spelling development trends	spelling is mostly correct- ✓ needs rule for affect/effect
AUDIENCE AWARENESS	
Language addresses intended audience	✓ decidedly
Focuses on topic	✓ yes
Uses varied vocabulary	✓ yes
Organizes text logically	✓ - yes - clear intro/definite ending
Relates sentences to each other	✓ strong transition of ideas
Writes in logical sequence	✓ yes
Aware of genre conventions (narrative, descriptive, explanatory, (persuasive))	- personalizes statements - interacts with reader

Instructional Needs

needs instruction in the use of paragraphing
spelling needs- affect/effect use

Seven-year-old Gary came to us as a beginning writer. His first composition was a story about himself. Like most beginning writers, he used the same sentence patterns again and again when he wrote nonfiction text (see Figure 4.9).

FIGURE 4.9

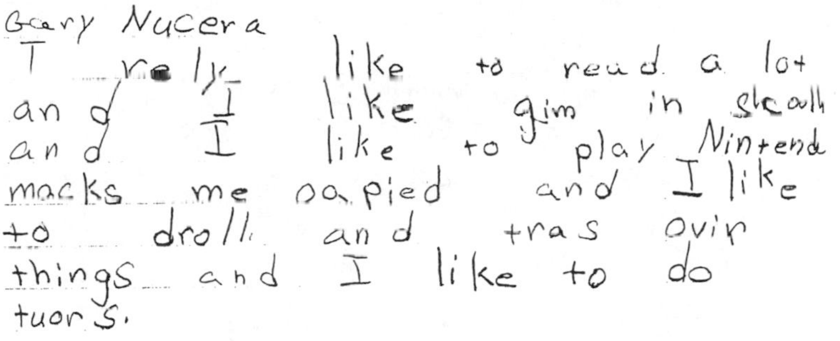

Gary Nucera
T re ly like to read a lot
an d I like gim in skoall
an d I like to play Nintend
macks me oa pied and I like
to droll and tras ovin
things and I like to do
tuor s.

Audience Awareness

After Gary listened to Steven Kellogg's *The Mysterious Tadpole*
he wrote the story that appears in Figure 4.10. He uses a variety of
syntax, maintains a clear focus, and shows an awareness of audience
which includes dialogue and story structure elements.

FIGURE 4.10

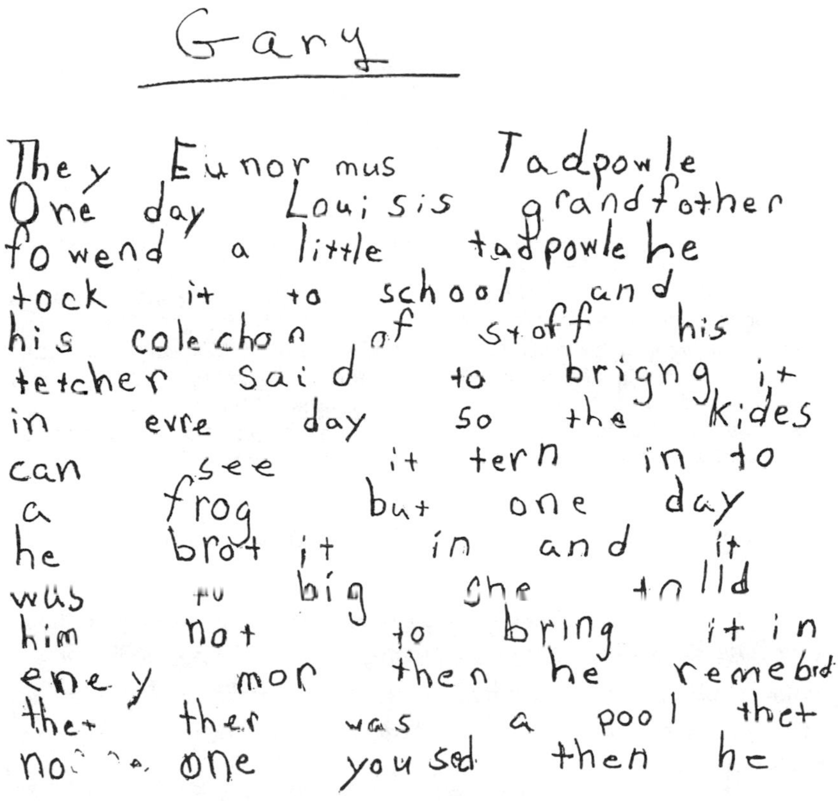

Gary

They Eunor mus Tadpowle
One day Louisis grandfother
to wend a little tadpowle he
tock it to school and
his colechon of stoff his
tetcher said to brigng it
in evre day so the kides
can see it tern in to
a frog but one day
he brot it in and it
was to big she tolld
him not to bring it in
eney mor then he remebrd
thet ther was a pool thet
no   one you sed then he

brot   him   ther   and
the   end   of   the yere   kides
went   to   swim   and
the   Tadpovle   came   up
and   scered   all   the   kides
a   way   the   swiming   pool
tetcher   told   him to   get
him   Out   of   here   then
he   tolld   his   liy   brareen
she   said   in   1862   ther
was   a   war   they   rented   a
boat   the   Tadpowle
was   ther   to   Louis   tolld
him   to   go   down   and
get   it   he   did   they got
he   llp   to   biuld   a   swimin-
pool.

One day, Louis' grandfather found a little tadpole. He took it to school and his collection of stuff. His teacher said to bring it in every day so the kids can see it turn into a frog. But one day he brought it in and it was so big she told him not to bring it in any more. Then he remembered that there was a pool that no one used. Then he brought him there and the end of the years kids went to swim and the tadpole came up and scared all the kids away. The swimming pool teacher told him to get out of here. Then he told his librarian. She said, "In 1862 there was a war." they rented a boat. The Tadpole was there too. Louis told him to go down and get it. He did. They got help to build a swimming pool.

Gary's sense of story structure (which can be assessed using Figure 6.6, p. 126) is developed as well. Most elements that make a story complete are included. His interactions with children's literature have helped him develop a strong relationship between knowledge of story and the ability to compose (Burke, 1990). Gary, as anticipated, has moved from the language of literature to a story of his own.

FIGURE 4.11

ASSESSING SENTENCE CONSTRUCTION

Child's Name *Gary*   Age *7*

Description of Sentence	Comments
Connects strings of ideas with "and" ("I love you and I have a dog and I go to school.").	*much less than in his expository writing*
Uses the same words to begin sentences. (" I like candy. I like apples." or "I have a sister. I have a brother. I have a bike.").	*not in this kind of writing*
Writes additions at the beginnings of sentences ("Today I went."). . . . . *most sentences*	*One day (often used)*
Writes simple sentences ("I went") with an addition ("to the park"); ("I ran after my friend").	*yes*
Uses dialogue ("He said, 'I don't think they're hungry.' ").	*yes*
Uses dependent clauses in sentences ("I like to eat candy when I am hungry.").	*not usually*
Combines sentences ("We went backstage and met them.").	*occasionally*
Uses coordinates in addition to "and" to connect sentences (but, or, so, yet, etc.) ("We rented a video but it was boring.").	*one sentence*
Uses descriptive words.	*yes*
Uses pronouns to identify people (clearly/) unclearly: "Mary and Jane were playing and she had to leave.").	
Uses a variety of sentence types. ("Why are they singing?" "Go home!").	*not yet*

Spelling Development

We review children's invented spellings in order to determine how they use the alphabet to represent their notions about the sounds letters represent. We review several samples of a child's spellings to determine trends that drive our instruction.

Gary, for example, felt comfortable inventing spellings. In his story in Figure 4.9, Gary wrote "macks" for "makes." His teacher noticed that in his journal, two other stories, and a letter he wrote the word "makes" the same way, "macks." She also noted that he invented spellings for other words that contained a silent "e" vowel marker. This trend guided his teacher to form a small instructional group with other children who needed to learn to use this silent vowel rule.

Our teachers review children's spelling trends regularly. They record these trends on the Spelling Trend Assessment sheet shown in Figure 4.12. The form provides a vehicle for reviewing spellings in a systematic format. It also provides the data necessary for planning instruction about spelling regularities and the idiosyncracies of the English language.

Unlike Gary, some beginning writers ask, "How do you spell _____?" We encourage these children to write without concern for spelling to develop their fluency with written language. Encouraging children to write so someone other than themselves can read it is also an important goal. Asking for correct spelling exhibits children's awareness of audience. Therefore, we sometimes supply words by writing them on four by six inch sheets of paper. Children save these, using strategies that help them to write the words from memory.

FIGURE 4.12

SPELLING TREND ASSESSMENT

Student's Spelling	Correct Spelling	Patterns Noted
macks	makes	silent "e"
tad powle	tad pole	addition/phonetic
colechon	collection	"tion" rule phonetic
tetcher	teacher	double vowel phonetic
brignng	bringing	omission "ing" rule
brot	brought	"ough" rule/omission
scered	scared	vowel subit.-phonel
ther	there	silent "e"
swimin	swimming	omission "ing" rule
Louisis	Louis's	possessive rule
to	too	omission /to/too rule
liybrareen	librarian	phonetic
fowend	found	phonetic
tern	turn	" "

Comments: Gary usually spells phonetically – as the word sounds. Rules for silent "e" and "ing" } Teach word cards – trace 3 a day. Spelling is age appropriate.

Spelling is: Mostly invented ✓ Somewhat correct ✓ Mostly correct___
Student writes: Using known words (seldom risks)____
　　　　　　　Using new words (risks) ✓
Sources of words: retelling + non-fiction
Student's Name: Gary　　　　　　Date: Feb, 91

Reporting Progress

Students' Participation In The Assessment Process

We have discovered, over the years, that when students are involved in assessing their growth, they take control of activities. They learn what they know, and are able to discuss what they need to learn. Because of our commitment to student-centered environments, we have developed a series of self-monitoring tools that are used by students. These appear throughout the text. Several are important for composition.

FIGURE 4.13

STUDENT'S COMPOSITION AND RETELLING CHECKLIST

NAME ___Gary_____ DATE ___-6-90_____

NAME OF COMPOSITION OR BOOK ___Story_____

AUTHOR ___Gary N._____

	YES	NO
SETTING:		
I began my composition/ retelling with an INTRODUCTION	✓	✓
I told WHEN the story happened	✓	
I told WHERE the story happened		✓
CHARACTERS: *Gary*		
I told about the main character	✓	
I told about the other characters *Fish puppy.*	✓	
PROBLEM: *Crab turtle*		
I told about the story problem or goal	✓	
EPISODES:		
I included episodes		✓
SOLUTION:		
I told how the problem was solved or the goal was met	✓	
I told how the story ended		
THEME:		
My story has a theme	✓	

When I compose/ retell on my own, I include: __Som characters__
__problum   problum and Salushin__

The next time I compose/ retell, I need to remember to include these things:_____
__yes I will punckshowe__
__wash on Marcks__

Figure 4.13, which was completed by Gary, has been used for self-assessment of story comprehension. This tool guided him to learn about his writing. In the initial conference with his teacher, Gary discovered that he could monitor his own composing. He found out that he included more than half of the elements in stories. This led him to the conclusion that, "Hey, I got most of them!"

The assessment conference, discussed in Chapter 7, can be replicated for composition. The same monitoring tool (see Figure 6.8, p. 129) includes all of the elements that are used to construct a cohesive story.

The more children write, the more often they begin to see the flip-flop nature of comprehension of story as it relates to composition. We recall the time that Jon discovered that his retelling self-monitoring tool could be used as an outline for writing his story. He ran to his teacher in the computer lab and whispered, "I'm cheating. Ya know what? I can look at this (showing her the Student's Composition and Retelling Checklist, Figure 6.8) to be sure that I included all of the things in a story that I write." We suggest that you review the retelling self-monitoring conference procedures in Chapter 7 in order to replicate the organizational procedures for composition.

Gary's teacher summarized her observations of his writing on the weekly Progress Report, Figure 4.14. Her descriptions match Gary's assessment.

A goal for our children and their teachers is to come to an agreement about what each knows and what each needs to do to grow. Figure 4.15, page 67, completed by eleven-year-old Maryann, displays one child's decision to use the teacher's monitoring sheet for reviewing her strengths and needs for writing.

Often children need the time to review their work alone or with peers. We have created several self-monitoring tools that meet specific needs. Figure 4.16, adapted from one developed by Glazer and Searfoss (1988, p. 144), was created so that youngsters learn to review their writing in order to see how they create text.

FIGURE 4.14

PROGRESS REPORT

Student's Name __Gary__　　Teacher's Name __Mrs. B.__

Time period: From: __I retelling from__ To: __listening — looking at writing of retelling__

AREA: (check one)　Comprehension __X__　Composition __X__　Vocabulary _____
　　　　Independence/Self-Esteem _____　Self-Monitoring _____

STRENGTHS	NEEDS (Questions)	PLANS
writes in logical order	**question** Will Gary produce as strong a sense of story when he creates his own ideas for text?	Have Gary compose a story on his own. Compare with his written retelling.
relates one sentence to the next	Will he retell in writing as fully when he reads rather than listens to a story?	Have Gary retell a story he has read on his own; in writing
uses a variety of sentence patterns	**needs** to become aware of appropriate use of punctuation	Read chorally with Gary. Note breath stops, compare with periods in the book.
writes in complete sentences	needs to specifically identify the problem and the solution in his written retelling.	Use the two sentence strategy for showing problem - solution
shows sense of audience awareness		Use word cards, three a day to trace.
usually uses a capital at beginning of sentence		
includes many story elements, character, setting, intro, ending, episodes.		

FIGURE 4.15

PROGRESS REPORT

Student's Name _Maryann_   Teacher's Name _Mrs. Nugent_

Time period: From: _Feb. 16_   To: _____

AREA: (check one) Comprehension_____   Composition_____   Vocabulary_____
                  Independence/Self-Esteem_____   Self-Monitoring_____

STRENGTHS	NEEDS (Questions)	PLANS
research with notecards		write questions
audience understands my writing	emprove supporting details	meet with my teacher for ideas
always use capitals, periods maybe commas	forget quotation marks lots	reread - find where quotes go
describing words - lots	better vocabulary	maybe use thesaurus or interesting word cards
intro episodes characters	endings are hard to do conclusions too	use story map try different endings make outline

One youngster, after using this sheet, said to her teacher, "Mrs. Belanger, I always write short sentences." The teacher concurred, and each went on with their tasks. At the end of the day, the same child approached her teacher and said, "Look, Mrs. Belanger, I decided to write one v-e-r-y long sentence. It has 57 words, and no periods." The self-monitoring tool guided the student to learn how to deliberately "carve" her text. The awareness permitted her to make a definite decision to change the format of her composition.

FIGURE 4.16

ABOUT MY WRITING

	COMMENTS
I have written all the ideas I want into my story.	*no*
I got my ideas from my own head, from brainstorming, from reading, from talking to other people, from interviewing...	✓
I included a beginning.	✓
I included a middle.	*sort of*
I included an ending.	*not yet*
I included episodes.	*of course*
When I read my story, I can close my eyes and have a picture in my head about the story.	*so so*
I think someone will be able to retell my story after they read it.	✓
I used one word to tell about an idea.	*sort of*
I wrote short sentences.	✓
I wrote long sentences.	✓
I wrote "and" lots of times in one sentence.	*no*
I used periods at the ends of sentences.	✓
I used capital letters at the beginning of sentences.	*all the time*
I think that people can read my handwriting.	*of course.*
I needed to use a typewriter or a computer because my handwriting is difficult to read.	*no way*
I reread my story to fix-up the spelling.	*not yet*
I reread my story and when my voice stopped I put a period at the end of that word.	✓

Adapted from Susan Mandel Glazer and Lyndon W. Searfoss, *Reading Diagnosis and Instruction: A C-A-L-M Approach.* Copyright © 1988.

In addition to looking at products, it is important that our children discover the behaviors—the processes—they engage in as they create their compositions. We encourage them to respond to the questions shown in Figure 4.17. We also create this sheet as a wall poster and hang it in obvious sections of the classroom.

FIGURE 4.17

PROCESSES I USE WHEN I COMPOSE

Name *Jon*

Date *April 23*

Title of My Writing *Ffight With Capt. J.C.*

1. What helped me to get the idea for this writing selection?

   I read a book about an inventor and I thought I could write a better story than that one.

2. How long have I been working on this piece of writing?

   three weeks

3. What gave me trouble while I was writing?

   I kept trying to add a problem to my story but it kept getting longer and there was no problem in it

4. What strategies did I use to revise drafts?

   I talked to my teacher but I still couldn't do it. My retelling of the invention story helped me.

5. What would I like to add or take away to make my writing better?

   I know I write a lot of things in my stories. I can't make it shorter yet.

6. How will I know when my writing is finished?

   When I run out of time I have to end the story.

7. Who is my audience for this writing?

   Every one who likes exciting stories.

FIGURE 4.18

Sadaf
    About My Writing
I like my writing because I write clearly.
I also like my writing because I leave
space and look in the diconary if I don't
know the words. Also I take my time
writing no matter what.

FIGURE 4.19

I do all kinds of writing.
In school we have writing
projects. For writing projects
I always do something different.
So far I have written realism,
description, animal stories, and
comedy. I have just recently
started comedy and I'm doing
very well.
    My favorite kind of writing
is fiction and animal
stories are what I find
easiest to write about.
Two recent animal stories
I have written are ~~Stormy~~
the ~~Seaweathering~~ Cat and
Martin ~~the~~ Warrior ~~the~~ Mouse.

good grades

    I write because I have
to or it is required. The
only times I enjoy writing
period is when I have
a brilliant brainstrom (often)
Also I'm excellent at writing
opening and ending. The middle

+

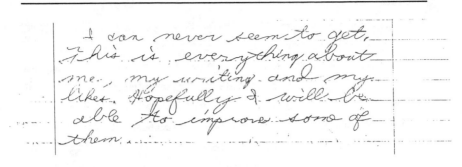

We use many formats as often as possible to encourage our children to look at their writing, beginning at age seven. Sadaf, a second grade student, and Jason, an eighth grader, were able to write about their compositions after two-and-one-half weeks of school. "I think you ought to read your composition and tell as much about how you've written it as you can," was the teacher's suggestion. Figures 4.18 and 4.19 are their responses to this suggestion.

An "Over Time" Review of Jonathan's Writing Development

Now that you've been introduced to our tools, we believe it is important to guide you through one student's long-term involvement with a creative piece of writing. Ten-year-old Jonathan agreed to share his nine-day efforts. The review, which we would have called a case study in earlier years, demonstrates the value of an ongoing daily assessment. It also illustrates how assessment drives instruction—how the instruction is altered based on the assessment process.

In previous writing efforts, Jonathan demonstrated his competence as a writer. He wrote, using a variety of syntactic structures, interesting combinations of words which made his text exciting to read. His teacher discovered after several creative efforts, however, that he had difficulty including a story problem and solution in his narratives. This trend emerged in his written retellings in response to reading literature, as well.

Jonathan usually preferred to use word processing to construct his original text. His initial draft illustrates that he used details and descriptive language. He seems to have a focus, writes in complete sentences, and uses a variety of syntactic structures. During a self-monitoring conference, Jonathan and his teacher decided that he had indeed included an introduction to his story, but had not yet included the details of the story setting and problem. Figure 4.20 shows Jonathan's first attempts and Figure 4.21 shows his self-monitoring. This self-assessment was carried out in conference with his teacher, Mrs. Belanger. Her assessment (see Figure 4.22) confirms Jon's self-assessment, and plans for appropriate instructional guidelines necessary to facilitate change. The conference spurred Jon to move, on his own, back to the computer.

FIGURE 4.20

```
    FLIGHT  WITH
         CAPT.  J.C.
    WELL   LET ME TELL
   YOU ABOUT HIM!HE
   HAS BEEN IN THE
   NAVY 9 YEARS & XHE HAS
   HAS BEEN IN THE AIR
   FORCE 10 YEARS!HE
   HAS HIS OWN PRIVATE
   PLANE,JET,HOT-AIR
   BALLOON,& A
   MINIATURE BLIMP.
   Now—LETS GO ON WITH
   THE STORY.
```

FIGURE 4.21

STUDENT'S COMPOSITION AND RETELLING CHECKLIST

NAME _Jon_   DATE _2/27_

NAME OF (COMPOSITION) OR BOOK _____

AUTHOR _me_

	YES	NO
SETTING:		
I began my composition/ retelling with an INTRODUCTION	✓	___
I told WHEN the story happened	✓	___
I told WHERE the story happened	✓	___
CHARACTERS:		
I told about the main character	___	___
I told about the other characters	___	___
PROBLEM:		
I told about the story problem or goal	___	Not 'tel'
EPISODES:		
I included episodes	Some	___
SOLUTION:		
I told how the problem was solved or the goal was met	___	✓
I told how the story ended	___	✓
THEME:		
My story has a theme	___	Not Yet

When I compose/ retell on my own, I include: _introduction, where when_

The next time I (compose)/ retell, I need to remember to include these things:_____
episodes

FIGURE 4.22

PROGRESS REPORT

Student's Name *Jonathan F.*   Teacher's Name *Belanger*

Time period: From:_____   To: *3/20*

AREA: (check one) Comprehension____ Composition____ Vocabulary____
Independence/Self-Esteem____ Self-Monitoring____

STRENGTHS	NEEDS (Questions)	PLANS
Conference elicited that Jon chooses to keep opening, stating it is an introduction. His wishes are respected.

He included where and when the story happened. Is beginning a sequenced series of events.
Uses descriptive words; several syntactic patterns, creating interesting language. Confirms audience awareness.
Demonstrates print awareness and prior knowledge of literature as seen in his use of expletives.
Conferencing is clearly beneficial as seen by his inclusion of setting and character name. | To begin to focus on theme or problem in this narrative. | Provide more writing opportunities focusing on story elements.
Prompt: what is the main character problem? |

    Student/teacher conferences, self-monitoring activities, and instructional guidelines were ongoing. On each self-monitoring sheet, he seemed to recognize that he had not yet included a problem or a solution. Jonathan was clearly aware that he needed to include a problem in his story. Ongoing assessment and monitoring continued to confirm this. It became clear to his teacher that a different instructional technique would be required to facilitate his including this story element.

His teacher decided to guide Jon to read and retell one of his favorite stories. The story was about a magician and his inventions. Jon was asked, in a conference, "What was the magician's problem?" He identified the problem. Then she asked, "Where's the problem in your story?" Jon sat for a few seconds, and then, as if a light bulb went off in his head, he grabbed the pencil and scribbled in the problem. He put it at the beginning of the story, as shown in Figure 4.23. (Note: We are showing the first out of six pages that Jon wrote before he went back and added the problem.) Then he used the self-monitoring sheet shown in Figure 4.24 to assess his composition

FIGURE 4.23

```
THE  STORY.  ONE          ← Performance Sample 2
FRIDAY  BEFOR  THE  20
DAY  WEEKEND.  I  WAS
ON  MY  WAY  TO
CAPT.J.C.'S  LAB—TO  HELP  HIM  LOOK
WHEN  ALL  OF  A       for his grandfather
SUDDEN  I  SAW  A    mysterious invention.
PERSON  FLYING  IN  A
WIERED  CONTRAPTION!
IT  WAS  CAPT.J.C.  &
HIS  NEW  INVENTION.
HOLY  @#%^&*$@$%%@!
  AS  SOON  AS  HE
```

His identifying the problem in the magician's story enabled him to create a problem in his own composition. This "Ah hah" experience was powerful. In later retellings and compositions, Jon consistently included the problem.

The quality, length, descriptive language, and details in Jon's first three drafts could easily have led his teacher to assume that he could complete the story without guidance. The important aspect of this child's samples is that without teacher guidance—direct prompting in an instructional conference—Jon would have written more episodes and never made closure by including a problem and its resolution.

FIGURE 4.24

STUDENT'S COMPOSITION AND RETELLING CHECKLIST

NAME _Jon_   DATE _3/20_

NAME OF (COMPOSITION)OR BOOK _____

AUTHOR _me_

	YES	NO
SETTING:		
I began my composition/ retelling with an INTRODUCTION	✓	—
I told WHEN the story happened	✓	—
I told WHERE the story happened	✓	—
CHARACTERS:		
I told about the main character	✓	—
I told about the other characters	✓	—
PROBLEM:		
I told about the story problem or goal	—	Not Yet
EPISODES:		
I included episodes	✓	—
SOLUTION:		
I told how the problem was solved or the goal was met	—	Not Yet
I told how the story ended	—	Not Yet
THEME:		
My story has a theme	—	Not Yet

When I compose/ retell on my own, I include: _setting, theme, plot introduction, lots of episodes._

_____

The next time I ~~compose~~ ~~retell~~, I need to remember to include these things:_____

problem and solve problem. I'm still working on the problem.

_____

Jon wrote several more times, completing his story (Figure 4.25) and self-monitoring sheet (Figure 4.26) about his writing. He cheerfully filled in his self-monitoring sheet, writing that nothing was now missing from the story.

FIGURE 4.25

```
    FLIGHT WITH
       CAPT. J.C.
   WELL   LET ME TELL
YOU ABOUT HIM!HE
HAS BEEN IN THE
NAVY 9 YEARS & HE
HAS  BEEN IN THE
AIR FORCE 10
YEARS!HE HAS HIS
OWN PRIVATE
PLANE,JET,HOT-AIR
BALLOON,& A
MINIATURE BLIMP.
  NOW LETS GO ON
WITH THE STORY. ONE
FRIDAY BEFOR THE ?0
DAY WEEKEND.I WAS
ON MY WAY TO
CAPT.J.C.'S LAB
TO HELP HIM LOOK
FOR HIS GREAT GREAT
GREAT GREAT
GRANDFATHER'S
MYSTERIOUS
INVENTION.
HE MADE IT 24 HOURS
BEFORE HE DIED AND
NOBODY KNEW WHAT IT
WAS & CAPT. J.C.
WANTED TO FIND IT
FIRST AND IF HE
DOES HE WILL GET 23
MILLION DOLLERS
FROM THE
GOVERNMET(I'LL GET
SOME TO).WHEN ALL
OF A SUDDEN I SAW A
PERSON FLYING IN A
WIERED CONTRAPTION!
IT WAS CAPT.J.C. &
HIS NEW INVENTION.
HOLY @#%^&*$@$%%@!
  AS SOON AS HE
HERED ME WHICH
PROBALY WASN'T THAT
HARD!HE TURNED
AROUNED   & SAID
HELLO & I JUST
STOOD THERE MOUTH
OPEN & WIDE EYED IN
AMAZEMENT. THEN HE
CAME DOWN FROM HIS
CONTRAPTION &
SLAPPED ME ACROSS
MY FACE (NOT THAT
HARD) TO GET ME OUT
OF MY TRANCE.THEN
HE TOOK ME TO HIS
```

LAB TO SHOW ME ALL
OF HIS INVENTIONS.
 WE WENT TO HIS LAB
WICH WAS ABOUT THE
SIZE OF THE MOON
(I'M EXAGGERATING)!
 HE SHOWED ME ALL
OF HIS INVENTIONS
WICH WERE SO.SO
INTERESTING! ONE OF
THE INVENTIONS WAS
A MINIATURE PLANE
THAT HAD NO WINDOWS
BUT YOU COULD SEE
OUT SIDE.I KNOW IT
SOUNDS WEIRD BUT IT
IS TRUE!DON'T ASK
ME HOW BUT IT'S
POSIBALE!HE SAID
IT'S A LARGE MIRROR
BUT INSTED OF
REFLECTING IT
ABSORBS WHAT IT
SEES.IT'S A MIRROR
 WITH LIKE MICRO-
CHIPS OR YOU COULD
PROBALY DISCRIBE IT
TO BE A GIANT
COMPUTER.THE
INTERIOR IS ALL A
BIG SCREAN.SO
WHEREVER YOU LOOK
YOU SEE THE
OUTSIDE.SO IF YOU
LOOK DOWN YOU WILL
SEE THE GROUND.IF
YOU LOOK UP YOU
WILL SEE CLOUDS.
I ASKED HIM WHAT
GAVE HIM THE
IDEA.HE REPLIED
IT'S A LONG STORY
SO I SAID NEVER
MIND.HE THEN
REMINDED ME WHAT I
WAS HERE FOR.BUT I
DIDN'T PAY ANY
ATENTION SO I JUST
KEPT LOOKING AROUND
WHEN ALLOF A SUDDEN
 I NOTICED A SMALL
INSTRUMENT. IT WAS
ABOUT THE SIZE OF A
FLY!CAPT.J.C. SAID
IT WAS A ROBOT FLY!
 HE SAID HE ALLWAYS
WANTED TO BE A FLY
AND SPY.SO I MADE A
REMOTE-CONTROL

MECHANICAL FLY YOU
CAN MAKE IT GO
ANYWHERE AND MAKE
IT GO IN ANY
DIRECTION AND THE
COMPUTER THAT
ENLARGES WHAT IT
SAW OR WHAT IT
SEES.THEN I
REMEMBERD WHY I WAS
HERE FOR SO WE
        STARTED
          THE
        SEARCH

FIRST WE TOOK ALL
OF HIS INVENTIONS
OUT WICH TOOK A
COUPLE HOURS MABY
EVEN LONGER.THEN WE
TOOK ALL OF THE
NUTS & BOLTS THAT
FFIL OUT OF SOME OF
HIS GISMOS.THEN
SWEPT THE ROOM THEN
MOPED IT TILL IT
WAS SO SHINY WHEN
THE SUN GLARED IT.
IF YOU LOOKED AT IT
IT HURTS YOUR EYES.
  NOW WE LOOKED FOR
ANY SECRET-PANELS.
THEN WHEN WE WERE
AT THE LAST SQUAR
ON THE WALL WE
PUSHED IT......THEN
IT MADE THE WHOLE
WALL TURN AROUND.
WE LOOKED ON THE
OTHER SIDE AND WE
SAW A BED THAT HAD
A WELL PRESERVED
BODY. AND THERE IN-
FRONT OF THE
BODY,ON A GOLD
STAND WAS THE GREAT
INVENTION GLEEMING
DUST-LESS.WE WERE
SO EXCITED WE TOOK
THE THING AND
WRAPED IT QUICKLY
AND RAN TO THE
MUSEUM TO GET IT ON
DISPLAY (NOT TO
MENTION WE WANTED
THE MONEY).WHEN WE
GOT THERE WE TOLD
THEM OUR NAMES AND

```
THEY KNEW US OF THE
TOP OF THEIR HEAD
AND TOOK THE
INVENTION AND CAME
BACK WITH THE
MONEY.
        THE END

    WAIT A MINUTE I
OR WE CAPT.J.C. AND
ME NEVER KNEW WHAT

THE INVENTION WAS!
AAAAA NEVER MIND.

        THE END

        BY,
        JONATHAN
          FERRANTE
```

FIGURE 4.26

STUDENT'S COMPOSITION AND RETELLING CHECKLIST

NAME _Jon_____ DATE _4/17_____

NAME OF COMPOSITION OR BOOK _Flight With Capt.J.C._

AUTHOR _Jon_____

	YES	NO
SETTING:		
I began my composition/ retelling with an INTRODUCTION	✓	—
I told WHEN the story happened	✓	—
I told WHERE the story happened	✓	—
CHARACTERS:		
I told about the main character	✓	—
I told about the other characters	✓	—
PROBLEM:		
I told about the story problem or goal	✓	—
EPISODES:		
I included episodes	✓	—
SOLUTION:		
I told how the problem was solved or the goal was met	✓	—
I told how the story ended	✓	—
THEME:		
My story has a theme	✓	—

When I compose/ retell on my own, I include: _everything_

_____

_____

The next time I (compose) ~~retell~~, I need to remember to include these things:_____

_nothing_____

Figure 4.27, 4.28, and 4.29 show his teacher's final assessments of Jon's progress in writing.

FIGURE 4.27

PROGRESS REPORT

Student's Name *Jonathan F.*   Teacher's Name *Belanger*

Time period: From:_____ To:____*4/17*_____

AREA: (check one) Comprehension_____ Composition __✓__ Vocabulary_____
Independence/Self-Esteem_____ Self-Monitoring_____

STRENGTHS	NEEDS (Questions)	PLANS
Jonathan has completed his story about Capt. J.C. The episodes toward the conclusion are focused to solve the problem and still continue to demonstrate good control of language and audience awareness. He seems to respond to questions asked, "How are your characters going to solve their problem?" "What are they going to do next?" Through the self-monitoring checklist Jon was able to identify all the elements of story within his own text.	Jon needs to eliminate or add ideas to clarify his narrative.	Jon will reread narrative to make additions or to eliminate text not supporting the story theme. Editing process will include: 1) rereading for punctuation 2) reread again to correct spelling.

FIGURE 4.28

Summary

Jon appears to be comfortable with the writing process as demonstrated by his enthusiasm and willingness to approach a writing task. Jon's written text contains a variety of syntactic patterns, including complex and sophisticated sentence structures.

He writes fluently and includes description and detail when he composes at the computer. He organizes text logically and uses appropriate vocabulary to convey the mood of the passage. Jon is an "emergent writer."

Jon's narrative writing includes a dialogue within the story as well as a dialogue with the audience. This technique captures the interest of the reader. He seems to have a focus for his story and is able to expand upon his ideas. He begins a narrative with an introduction and includes characters, episodes, and a setting. With conferencing and self-monitoring, Jon can be guided to include a problem and solution in his narrative.

He includes capital letters, punctuation, and general agreement of tense. An analysis of his spelling trends reveals that Jon usually spells words correctly with some transitional spellings, such as *hered* for *heard* and *probaly* for *probably*.

Recommendation:

As Jon continues in his writing of narratives, he should be guided to identify story structure elements within his writing with an emphasis on including *problem* and solution.

FIGURE 4.29

WRITING ASSESSMENT SUMMARY

Child's Name: _Jonathan_   Age: _9_

	Comments
WRITING STAGE	
Prewriting - (Scribbles, recognizes names and letters, spelling is prephonemic)	
Beginning - (Labels, requests help, repeats sentence patterns, invents spelling)	
Emergent - (purposeful in writing, focuses thoughts, varies content, spelling is conventional)	
SENTENCE CONSTRUCTION	
Writes one word sentences	
Repeats sentence patterns	
Varies sentence structure	yes
Uses other elements of syntax for creating interesting text	uses expletives, dialogue, lots of descriptive language appropriate to topic
MECHANICS	
Handwriting is legible	computer used
Uses punctuation: (periods) (commas) other) *some*	some quotation marks used
Uses capitalization	N/A - all story in caps
Spelling development trends	mostly correct, some double vowels "ea"-heard, "ie", "e"-weird
AUDIENCE AWARENESS	
Language addresses intended audience	yes, uses dialogue
Focuses on topic	yes
Uses varied vocabulary	yes, appropriate to topic
Organizes text logically	yes, some elaboration - can confuse audiences
Relates sentences to each other	definitely
Writes in logical sequence	yes
Aware of genre conventions (narrative,) descriptive, explanatory, persuasive)	strong sense of story

Instructional Needs

Needs instruction in use of paragraphs and dialogue - needs help in narrowing focus, elaborates beyond immediate theme.

Jon's teacher, at the end of the reporting period, wrote the following letter to him. He read it, asked the teacher questions, and then handed it to his parents at the parent/student/teacher conference. The letter was as follows.

Dear Jon,

You love to write. I know that because you write as much as you can. Your compositions demonstrate your enthusiasm and eagerness to produce stories for others to read.

You are an emergent writer. That means, Jon, that you write fluently. You include lots of description and details. You do this by using many adjectives in your stories. You create many different kinds of sentences as well. If you look at your Captain J.C. story, you will see that you have used adverbs, words that tell where the story happens, at the beginning of sentences. Other times you begin with nouns or pronouns. These are words that tell the names of the people in the story. Sometimes you use dialogue, which helps your reader hear the people in the story talk. We found out that you use very interesting words, and that makes your story fun to read.

After writing five drafts, you discovered that you still needed to include Captain J.C.'s problem. We sat together and read and retold the story about a magician. Do you remember it? Well, after that conference you were able to write the Captain's problem, and finish your story.

We will continue to work on including problems and solutions to problems in your stories.

You've learned a lot this reporting period.

Love,

Mrs. Belanger, Your teacher

Summary

We attempted to demonstrate several procedures used by our teachers and students for assessing writing. We have discussed writing as a development process. We've included procedures for nurturing this development as appropriate.

Five factors remain of prime importance:

1. Writing is developmental; progress in writing growth will occur in those areas that are ready to be developed.

2. Many opportunities for writing must be continuous and ongoing.

3. Writing growth occurs when teachers act as facilitators and guides, conferencing with students as necessary.

4. Writing growth occurs when students participate in the assessment process, recognizing their own strengths and needs.

5. Finally, teachers and children, together, must move back and forth between assessment and instruction in flip-flop activity as the need occurs.

5 Assessing Comprehension Processes

What are Think-alouds?

When readers produce think-alouds, they read a portion of text and say out loud what they are thinking as they try to make sense of it. Then they read more, think aloud again, and continue. This thinking aloud reveals part of their reading-thinking behaviors when they are in the process of reading. The results help guide our instructional decisions.

Think-alouds focus our attention on HOW readers are comprehending. The following examples, made by two fourth grade girls, show their differing responses to the same sentence. Consider how these think-alouds might affect instruction for each of these students. Liz looks at the sentence and reads:

> "My dog was stealing up on the infant sparrow when, abruptly, an old black-chested bird fell like a stone right in front of the dog's face, and, with all its feathers standing on end, uttering a desperate chirp, it hopped once and then again in the direction of the dog's open jaw." Then she says, with a quizzical look, "Well, I'm not sure about this...I'm not sure what this 'stealing' means. But there was a baby sparrow in a nest and there was a black bird that fell in front of the dog's face, and the dog wanted to eat it. And it was coming in the direction of the dog (pause). Why?"

Liz's think-aloud demonstrates that she has worked hard to understand this text. She knows what she understands, and she is alert to what confuses her. She is aware of reasons for reading, revealing purposeful interactions with text.

Would we have known this about Liz's reading if we had followed the common practice of asking post-reading questions? Perhaps, if her answers were rich in detail and forthcoming about her reading-thinking processes. But this think-aloud and others she has made reveal a reader active in her quest for meaning and metacognitively aware. When her teacher asks her how she feels about making think-alouds, Liz answers, "It's easy. I just say what's in my head." Then she adds, "Sometimes I don't know things are there until I say them. Sometimes it helps me to know what I know."

Anne, on the other hand, struggles with this same sentence. After reading aloud, she says, "Was it this bird fell and died? Why was he going to a dog's open jaw?" She then quickly moves on to the next sentence, asks another question using words that closely paraphrase the text, and does not attempt to answer it. When she finally reaches the end, she says, "I don't get it."

Anne's think-alouds illustrate that she is less in control than Liz. The minimal control indicates that she is less purposefully involved and probably inefficient in her ability to find meaning. Anne does not know what to do when she does not understand what she reads.

"I don't usually get it until the teacher asks questions. Then sometimes I can figure out what she wants," Anne says about her reading. When Anne talks about making think-alouds, she says, "It's OK. Sometimes they help me figure out what it's about."

"How do they do that?" I ask.

"They make me think about it more," she replies.

Are these readers benefiting from thinking aloud? Both girls talk about knowing that think-alouds slow down their reading. However, these students say that when they slow down and take more time, they understand the text better. Anne, particularly, profits from taking time.

Why Should We Use Think-alouds to Assess Comprehension?

When students think aloud, we hear what they attend to as they are reading. Once we understand, we can make decisions about instruction for them. Anne, for example, needs help noticing when she is confused. She needs encouragement to do something about resolving her confusions. She could predict, hypothesize, visualize, recall things she knows that relate, or respond in a number of other ways. But she needs to know that she can do something.

We recommend think-alouds, in addition to post-reading activities like retelling (see Chapter 6) for several reasons. The think-aloud process—stopping after each sentence to say one's thoughts about text—relies on immediate feelings, attitudes, opinions, information access, and reasoning. We can also ask students to tell about their thinking after the reading is completed. However, when students report about how they understood a text after reading, they rely on their memories. When this happens, students may say what they believe teachers expect, instead of talking about their actual thinking (Afflerbach & Johnston, 1984; Ericsson & Simon, 1980). We feel that information about how students think as they try to understand text helps us to plan effective instruction.

Think-alouds tap *current* thinking. We use think-alouds along with the other strategies mentioned in our text to learn about our students' reading. Alternative forms of assessing provide us with an understanding of the subtleties for instructional needs. Some of the advantages of think-alouds are that they:

- show some of readers' in-process thinking;
- simultaneously slow down reading and encourage thinking about text;
- help us understand what confuses readers;
- guide our planning for instruction;
- reveal to students who are working with peers how others think as they read.

How Have Others Used Think-alouds?

As long ago as 1908, Huey asked students to talk out loud about how they understood vocabulary words. Other researchers interested in reading-thinking processes have used think-aloud procedures as readers respond to poetry (Kintgen, 1985), second language learning (Hosenfeld, 1979), and readers' use of the formats for various genres (Olson, Mack & Duffy, 1981). These researchers and others have provided us with justification for using think-alouds to help us understand student in-process thinking while reading diverse formats.

Rummelhart (1977), and Collins, Brown, and Larkin (1980), considered research pioneers in the study of how readers construct meanings as they read, used think-alouds in their investigations. They spurred many to continue research on reading processes (A. Brown, 1980; Palincsar & Brown, 1984; Bereiter & Bird, 1985). Davey (1983), C. Brown (1988), Brown and Lytle (1988), Russavage and Arick, (1988), Wilson and Russavage (1989), and others have explored the use of think-alouds in classrooms. Hynds (1989), for example, used think-alouds to investigate and encourage adolescents' response to literature in collaborative group work. These teacher/researchers found ways to create strategies for helping students figure out what to do to understand text. Instructional strategies extended research into teaching.

Using Think-alouds in Classrooms

How To Get Started

To begin, you need to consider some issues that relate to using think-alouds. These include (1) what text to use; (2) whether to save the think-aloud; (3) directions to students; and (4) what settings to use. We have solved some of these problems in the following ways. You may find your own solutions as you use think-alouds with your own students.

Selecting a Text

Students can make think-alouds from any text: texts that are easy or difficult, short or long, familiar or unfamiliar. The choice of text will influence students' think-alouds. When our students choose the text, they feel in control and are comfortable. This usually results in their thinking more about the text than when our teachers choose the texts. We encourage our children and teachers to make think-alouds with their science and social studies texts as well as with literature ones, for they are familiar with the format of these already.

Our students often think aloud during conferences with their teacher as they begin a new section or chapter of their books. This helps us learn about how each student processes ideas in the specific text. We find out if they relate previous ideas to the new ones, if they notice titles and subtitles in nonfiction texts, if they form opinions about the text, and if they think about the text in other ways.

The texts students use for think-alouds should be challenging for them. If a text is easy for readers, they often say "um hum" or "OK" and move on quickly, not revealing much of their thinking. This may indicate to us that their thinking processes work automatically when they understand the text (Afflerbach & Johnston, 1984).

Our texts for think-alouds are from eight to twenty sentences long. We find that a shorter text may not allow students to develop an idea. Texts that are too long discourage students and tire them out.

Students' interest and prior knowledge about a text affect what they say in their think-alouds. Since we know that these issues are central to understanding, assessing their abilities to use these can guide our decisions about what to teach them. For example, in the think-aloud below, a first grader named John loses interest in a text even though he has chosen it. As a single instance, this would not be meaningful. However, John's teacher used it to illustrate this frequent behavior of his. She is reading to him from *How Things Work* (1982).

"Some new kinds of musical instruments have no strings, no tubes, and nothing to tap or hammer on," read his teacher aloud.

John said, "Oh those kinds go" (blew puffs of air with his mouth).

"These instruments use an electrical current to make special sounds," his teacher continued.

"Um, I'm not thinking about that. I'm thinking about the toys I want," John said

His teacher noted in a summary that, "For John, the comprehension process is often disrupted by shared focus and avoidance behaviors."

Saving Data from Think-alouds

Sometimes we save our students' think-alouds by taping them. Then we either transcribe the tape or listen to it and take notes. Sometimes we listen as students make think-alouds and take notes right then. Sometimes we listen without trying to save what they are saying at all. Our students each have their own tape for an entire reporting period, on which they record their retellings and think-alouds. Students constantly record work, sitting in corners or hallways alone or with a friend. Our teachers, parent volunteers, or aides do the transcribing, or we listen to the tape and take notes as we listen.

Directions to Students

We begin think-alouds by saying, "I am interested in what you think about as you read. So I'd like you to read a sentence and then say out loud what you are thinking as you work at understanding the text." Saying more at this point can inappropriately direct students' thinking, and thus control the content of their think-aloud (Afflerbach & Johnston, 1984). If they are silent, we simply say, "What are you thinking about now?" or "Don't forget to think out loud."

Some children read out loud and then think aloud. Others choose to read to themselves. Either way, the mode for reading is best decided by each student. The choice will happen NATURALLY.

Our teachers sometimes model thinking aloud, using it as an instructional strategy. They do this when they read stories to their students. During reading they pause, look up from the book, use a different tone of voice, and "think aloud" about an idea from the text. Sometimes they point to their heads to indicate that the ideas they are sharing come from them and not the book.

We often remind students to think aloud at the end of each sentence. Some students can't stop, and keep reading. Our teachers remind the children that it is important to stop at sentence ends, for that is the best way to learn about how they think about text. Some of our teachers prefer to let students who want to do so stop at paragraph or subtitle-endings in passages. Students can make think-alouds in this manner. However, we caution these teachers that reading too much results in responses that are retrospective; students are telling what they remember rather than providing information about their in-process activities.

Our directions usually include asking our students to read the text aloud before they think about it. This is not necessary to making a think-aloud, and may even distract older readers. With our younger readers, however, it helps us to know where they are in the text, reveals mispronunciations, and gets oral communication started. Once they read aloud, thinking aloud frequently follows easily.

Settings for Think-alouds

Our students make think-alouds by themselves or with someone listening. Thinking aloud is initially easier for some readers if there is an audience; however, more is learned about the reader if the listener does not talk or interfere with the reader.

Figure 5.1 summarizes the use of think-alouds in several settings. This framework helped one teacher to realize that students working collaboratively were able to make group think-alouds. This usually happens when all read the same portion of text and then share with each other what they are thinking about. When this occurs, the assessment flip-flops to instruction, since they model their thinking for one another. Our teachers try to notice the kinds of contributions each student makes, in much the same way they notice student contributions to group discussions. Many sit apart from the group, listen, and jot observations down on Post-It notes.

FIGURE 5.1

Why Use Think-alouds in Different Contexts?

Alone
- to help yourself understand difficult text
- to tape record for someone else (for assessment purposes, as a model for use in a listening center, or as part of a class study on "How We Read"

With a peer:
- to help each other understand difficult text
- to model your thinking for your partner (for teaching purposes)

With a teacher
or an aide:
- to show how you think when you read (for assessment purposes)
- to share a favorite part of a text (as part of a reading conference)

With a group:
- to help each other understand difficult text
- to share how you think when you read

Assessing Think-alouds

Once you collect a think-aloud, you need to decide how to look at it for information. Many different frameworks have been used to examine think-aloud data. As you use think-alouds, and become familiar with the kinds of things your students say, you will find your own ways of describing their thinking.

We use a modification of an analytic system originally developed for research purposes by Lytle (1982). As we work with students of varying ages and reading abilities, we try to account for the kinds of thinking they do in response to text. The reading-thinking behaviors we look for include: restates text ideas; adds own ideas; recognizes when doesn't understand; rereads; recalls prior knowledge; notices the writing; hypothesizes, predicts, or reasons; and forms opinions. Our Record of Think-aloud sheet, shown in Figures 5.3 and 5.5, illustrates this system for looking at think-aloud data.

No student uses all the categories on this sheet, particularly when reading any one text. We hope that eventually our students use a variety of thinking strategies to understand text. Therefore, it is important that we notice whether our students use many of these categories over time and with different texts.

When we analyze think-alouds, we also attend to two issues: what our students usually do when they don't understand, and whether they are able to connect ideas in order to understand the whole. These concepts can be analyzed only after several samples have been reviewed. We assess think-aloud data in this way in narrative summaries, as shown in Figure 5.11 on page 108.

Sample Think-alouds

A first grader. Figure 5.2 is part of a think-aloud made near the end of the year by Brian, a first grader. His responses to the text are highlighted in the comments surrounding the think-aloud and are noted on the Record of Think-aloud sheet in Figure 5.3. As you can see, Brian uses a variety of thinking to understand this text.

Brian and his teacher were sitting side by side, holding Mercer Mayer's *There's A Nightmare in My Closet* (1968) between them and looking at it together. Brian's teacher helped him pronounce words he did not recognize, and these are shown in brackets. Sometimes our teachers even read the text aloud to a student, who then thinks aloud about the sentences after he has listened to them.

We find that our young readers often draw us into talking with them about the text as they make think-alouds. This is a natural way to interact during reading. If we are using the think-aloud for assessment purposes, we try to respond to the student naturally but not say too much. We need to be careful not to add new ideas or guide the student's thinking about the text. Brian's teacher talks to him several times in figure 5.2, but does not direct how he thinks about this text with her comments. After Brian finished thinking aloud about the first few pages of this book, his teacher read the rest of it to him.

On the Record of Think-aloud sheet, Brian's teacher has checked behaviors that Brian used to help himself understand this text. Sometimes our teachers use the spaces on this sheet to check behaviors in this way, and sometimes they keep a tally of the number of times a student uses these behaviors. Sometimes they use the spaces to write in examples from the think-aloud.

A fourth grader. Figure 5.4 is part of the think-aloud produced by a fourth grade girl named Anne. She is reading the beginning of George's *Julie of the Wolves* (1972), which she reads slowly and correctly.

FIGURE 5.4

Think-Aloud of a Fourth Grader

1. **Miyax pushed back the hood of her sealskin parka and looked at the Arctic sun.**

Why did she look at the sun?

2. **It was a yellow disc in a lime-green sky, the colors of six o'clock in the evening and the time when the wolves awoke.**

I don't know.

3. **Quietly she put down her cooking pot and crept to the top of a dome-shaped frost heave, one of the many earth buckles that rise and fall in the crackling cold of the Arctic winter.**

Why did she put down her cooking pot?

4. **Lying on her stomach, she looked across a vast lawn of grass and moss and focused her attention on the wolves she had come across two sleeps ago.**

Why did she pay attention to the wolves?

5. **They were wagging their tails as they awoke and saw each other.**

Why were they wagging their tails?

This think-aloud illustrates a behavior that Anne uses frequently in her think-alouds. She asks a question; here, four questions. The language used in her questions closely paraphrases the text. She also does not attempt to answer any of them. Her response in sentence 2, "I don't know," is another frequent response of Anne's to text. These are noted on the Record of Think-aloud shown in Figure 5.5.

FIGURE 5.5

RECORD OF THINK-ALOUD

Child's Name ___Anne___   Age ___11___

Text Read ___"Julie of the Wolves"___   Date ___10/7___

Directions: Place a check, tally, and/or write down examples of student's use of these reading-thinking behaviors.

	FREQUENTLY	SOMETIMES
Restates text ideas: -paraphrases	✓ Asks questions	
-summarizes		
-uses own words		
Add own ideas		
Recognizes when doesn't understand: -words		
-sentences	✓ (maybe)	
-larger ideas		
Rereads		
Recalls prior knowledge		
Notices writing of text		
Hypothesizes, predicts, or reasons about text ideas		
Forms opinion about ideas or writing		
Other		

On the Reporting Progress sheet shown in Figure 5.6, Anne's teacher writes that when Anne is confused she does nothing about it. She also writes that Anne is not connecting the ideas of the text so that she understands the whole. Since this is Anne's third think-aloud, her teacher noticed these patterns in her responses to text. She also notes that she selected this text for the think-aloud, and that Anne should select the next one herself.

FIGURE 5.6

PROGRESS REPORT

Student's Name __*Anne*__   Teacher's Name __*Carol*__

Time period: From: __*Sept.*__   To: __*Dec.*__

AREA: (check one) Comprehension __✓__   Composition____   Vocabulary____
               Independence/Self-Esteem____   Self-Monitoring____

STRENGTHS	NEEDS (Questions)	PLANS
Anne successfully makes think-alouds. She says that she "doesn't have much" in her head when she reads. She mainly: -paraphrases -says "I don't know"	How can I help her to -connect ideas + get a sense of the whole? -do something when she doesn't understand?	Use lots of encouragement. Continue reading fiction. Use her book. Make think-alouds with a partner.

A seventh grader. In Figure 5.7, Barbara, a seventh grader, makes a think-aloud from the beginning of Avi's *A Man Named Poe* (1991). Here she draws on previous knowledge she has of New York City, visualizes the scene, and notices the function of the writing ("it's description"). Her tentativeness, shown by her frequent use of "might be," illustrates her understanding of the range of possible subjects that this text could be about. She is able to select an interpretation and continue, exploring whether it makes sense as she reads. She also acknowledges when she does not understand something. When this happens in sentence 6, she thinks about the writing as one way of handling her uncertainty. Barbara's think-aloud shows her as a confident, competent reader with this text.

FIGURE 5.7

Think-Aloud of a Seventh Grader
"A Man Named Poe"

1. **The old city lay dark and cold.**
   Might be at night and it's cold.
2. **A raw wind whipped the street lamps and made the gas flames hiss and flicker like snake tongues.**
   Might be a storm brewing and like street lamps are just like going back and forth just 'cause the wind is so strong. It's like the gas flames, they're going on and off. They're kind of like when your electricity goes off, it goes like on and off.
3. **Fingers of shadow leaped over sidewalks, clawing silently upon closely set wooden houses.**
   People like walking down a sidewalk and there would be clouds going over the houses.
4. **Stray leaves, brittle and brown, rattled like dry bones along the cold stone gutters.**
   This might be in fall when the leaves are all dried out and how they just bang against each other and it makes like a rattling noise.
5. **A man, carpetbag in hand, made his way up college hill, up from the sluggish river basin, battling the steep incline, the wind, and his own desire.**
   He's trying to fight the wind, like going upstairs, and the wind is trying to bring him back down this. He might be trying to get inside somewhere. That's why he's going up there.
6. **He was not big, this man, but the old army coat he wore — black and misshapen, reaching to below his knees — gave him an odd bulk.**
   He wasn't big or tall, he's just like regular size, and the author's describing what he wore and all his actions that he did and (pause) expressions. Like, "gave him an odd bulk." Well I'm not sure what they means, actually, but it's description.

The influence that think-alouds can have on instruction is illustrated in Barbara's response to sentence 3. After listening to this response, her teacher decided to guide her to learn about figurative language. They looked back at this example together, and located several others in this text. Barbara easily understood what figurative language was. When she reread this sentence, she knew that no one except the main character was walking down this sidewalk.

A fourth grader reading nonfiction text. In Figure 5.8, Emily is reading the beginning of a chapter about the Age of Inventions in a social studies text (King & Anderson, 1980). She is considering using this in her report about the cotton gin. In this think-aloud, Emily uses reading-thinking behaviors she has used previously with narrative texts. Her first response after reading the sentence is to paraphrase it. Then she thinks about the text in other ways. (The comments surrounding the think-aloud highlight her thinking with this text.)

It is interesting to notice that Emily makes no distinction between reading narratives and reading this nonfiction text. She says nothing in response to the title, and does not use it at all to help herself understand the rest of the text. She uses thinking behaviors here that she uses with fiction; we will have Emily make think-alouds from other nonfiction texts and see if these patterns remain.

Sometimes we ask our students to listen to their think-aloud and use the self-assessment sheet shown in Figure 5.9. When she filled this out, Emily listened to her tape and checked those behaviors on the "What I Did" side that she thought she used. She also responded to "How It Helped" by checking that side.

FIGURE 5.8

**Think-Aloud of a Fourth Grader Reading Nonfiction
"Eli Whitney's Invention"**

1. **Eli Whitney's Invention**

   (no response)

   Paraphrases; Hypothesizes 2. **Eli Whitney had a plan for a new way to make guns.**

   So she was going to make guns. For people or for the stores.

3. **First, though, he needed to hire workers and buy machines.** *Revises Hypothesizes*

   So he had to buy machines and hire workers to help him make the guns. (pause) He's a man.

4. **So Whitney decided to ask the government for money to try his idea.**

   Ask a question So that the government might give him the money so he could do his idea. If it works, then well even if it doesn't work, he'll have to pay them back anyway, right?

   I guess so.

5. **Guns, like everything else at that time, were made by hand.**

   Predicted So if he would invent a machine that makes the guns he would make a lot of money and it would be a lot faster. Because I would think it would take awhile by hand.

6. **A gunsmith made each part separately and fitted the parts together.**

   Hypothesizes So it must have took a lot of concentration. Especially if you had to make one of those small parts, if you were one of the people.

FIGURE 5.9

ABOUT MY THINK-ALOUDS

Name *Emily*
Date *January 21*
Title *the Age of Inventions*

WHAT I DID	always	sometimes	never	a lot	a little	not at all
				HOW IT HELPED		
As I was reading. . .						
I restated what it said by						
-paraphrasing		X		X		
-summarizing						
-using my own words						
I added my own ideas		X		X		
I noticed when I didn't understand						
-a word						
-a sentence						
-a larger idea						
I reread						
I remembered other things I know		X		X		
I looked at the way it was written						
I hypothesized or predicted						
I formed an opinion about the text		X			X	
I. *asked questions.*		X			X	
I liked this text					X	

Usually students need to do this with their teacher the first few times, so that they understand what the categories mean and how to self-monitor using the check sheet. Some students listen to their tape alone and others do it with a partner. This spurs discussions about what they hear and how they feel about it. Younger students may not be able to understand how to self-monitor think-alouds. When they are able, however, using a self-monitoring check sheet becomes a useful instructional activity for helping students think about their thinking behaviors when they read.

Reporting Progress

We report think-aloud data in three ways: summary charts, narrative summaries by teachers, and student summaries.

Summary Charts

When students make a number of think-alouds, we record them on a Summary of Think-alouds sheet. Figure 5.10 shows one filled out for Anne's think-aloud work over a reporting period. As time progressed, she gradually used more categories. Some of our teachers and students like to have a visual representation of think-aloud work. This and the retelling graph (see Chapter 6) provide means for noting progress over time.

FIGURE 5.10

SUMMARY OF THINK-ALOUDS

F = frequently
S = sometimes

Name __Anne__

Date	Title	Restates text ideas:	-paraphrases	-summarizes	-uses own word	Add own ideas	Recognizes when doesn't understand: -words	-sentences	-larger ideas	when confused: Rereads	Recalls prior knowledge	Notices writing of text	Hypothesizes, predicts, or reasons about text ideas	Forms opinion about ideas or writing	Other-questions
9/10	Mother Sparrow	F								F					F
4/24	The Man Who Was Poe	F								F					F
10/15	Gibraltar's Barbary Apes	S	S										S		S
11/5	The Wolves of Willoughby Chase	S	S				S			S		S	S		S
11/20	Eli Whitney's New System			S			S					S			
12/4	Call It Courage			S	S					S	S	S	S		
12/18	Jonathan Livingston Seagull			S	F	S			S	S	S		S	S	

Narrative Summaries by Teachers

All of our teachers write narrative summaries of their students' work. If students have used think-alouds, they are included in these narratives. Figure 5.11 is a summary of Anne's think-aloud work. It restates information shown in Figure 5.10.

FIGURE 5.11

Narrative Summary of Think-aloud Work for Anne

Anne has made think-alouds based on six narrative texts and two expository texts during this reporting period. She now successfully verbalizes her thoughts while reading.

Initially, Anne spent much time paraphrasing the text. She also frequently asked questions, using wording directly from the text. She never sought answers to these questions.

Now, Anne's reading-thinking behaviors center more on her interpretations of the text. She often summarizes, using her own words. She visualizes scenes from the reading, and she incorporates prior knowledge. She sometimes thinks about the writing, commenting on sentence structure and word choice.

At times Anne hypothesizes and predicts to help herself project what an entire segment of text is about. Anne says when she does not understand an idea.

Future work could focus on encouraging Anne to acknowledge ideas that she does not understand. Once she is able to say, "I don't know," she can be guided to use the various think-aloud strategies to help herself make meaning of text. She should also be tentative in interpreting text, saying "Maybe," or "It might be."

Figure 5.12 shows the think-aloud portion of a narrative summary for Diane, who made two think-alouds during this reporting period. Her teacher writes about her response to the think-alouds, and later integrates this information into other reporting about Diane's reading comprehension.

FIGURE 5.12

Think-aloud Portion of Progress Report for Diane

In examining Diane's thoughts as she made think-alouds, it was apparent that she paraphrased and that she was able to retain a sense of the beginning of the passage as she continued reading. Diane's ability to summarize and to predict are also two useful strategies. However, when she came to a word that she did not immediately recognize, she would say, "Um, nothing comes to my head." It seemed that she did get some meaning, though, because she picked up her train of thought in the next sentence. Although she had an overall sense of the passage, her concern for individual words interfered with her confidence and her comprehension. She should work on strategies for thinking about unknown words.

Figure 5.13 is an example of one portion of a narrative report that discusses think-aloud data. Joe made only one think-aloud, and his teacher uses information from it to continue her discussion of his comprehension processes.

FIGURE 5.13

Think-aloud Portion of Progress Report for Joe

Joe was asked to make a think-aloud from the beginning of *The Call of the Wild* by Jack London. After each sentence, Joe told what he was thinking about as he read. This demonstrated that Joe paraphrases sentences and sometimes summarizes, combining ideas from previous sentences. He is also aware of when he does not understand a word or a sentence. At one point, he reread when he did not understand. It seemed that he recalled prior knowledge, as he mentioned Antarctica after he read about the cold climate of the north. It was possible that he makes pictures in his mind, because he often said "I see" before telling his thoughts about a sentence. All of these are strategies that can help Joe understand text. In a few instances, when he realized that he did not understand, he did nothing to help himself comprehend the text.

We do not ask all of our students to make think-alouds for assessment purposes. We use think-alouds to examine students' reading-thinking behaviors when we are puzzled about their reading processes. Sometimes we use think-alouds when we want more information to confirm or discard hunches about how a student is thinking as he or she reads.

We also write letters to our students that report on our work together. The following letter was written to Anne by her teacher at the end of a reporting period where she made many think-alouds.

> Dear Anne,
>
> You have become successful at saying aloud your thoughts as you are reading. I can tell this because you have made many think-alouds in this reporting period.
>
> In the beginning, you showed that you were mostly asking questions using words right out of the text. You asked lots of questions without answering them.
>
> Now when you read, I can tell from your think-alouds that you ask a question and try to answer it, with information from the book or from your head. You also think about the text in many other ways. Now, you picture scenes from the book in your head. You also tell what you think certain ideas mean. Sometimes you form opinions about the ideas in the text.
>
> I hope you will work on two things: 1) noticing when you do not understand something, and 2) doing something about helping yourself figure out what it might mean. Try out several different meanings if you can. Then you can choose the one you like best, after you've read some more of the text.
>
> Keep working hard on thinking a lot when you read. I am glad we could work together on think-alouds.
>
> Love,
> Your teacher, Mrs. Abitabilo

Student Summaries of Think-aloud Work

We believe in having students participate in assessment processes often and in varied ways. The sheet for Self-assessment of Think-aloud Work is one way that students can look at their reading-thinking processes over time. Even if they have not used the "What I Did and How It Helped" sheet shown in Figure 5.9, they often answer these three questions about their use of think-alouds.

Figure 5.14 was filled in by Anne, the fourth grader whose work is shown and analyzed in figures 5.4, 5.5, 5.6, 5.10, and 5.11. She is perceptive about her self-assessment and her goals for further work.

FIGURE 5.14

SELF-ASSESSMENT OF THINK-ALOUDS

Name *Anne*   Date *July*

Teacher *Amanda*

1. Here's how I feel about making think-alouds:

   Sometimes I like them because it helps me to think.

2. The best part about my think-alouds is when I

   answer a question I have.

3. The part about my think-alouds that I want to change is

   try to think about lots of answers – not just one.

Figure 5.15 was filled in by Brian, the first-grader whose think-aloud is in Figure 5.2. His teacher filled this in for him as they talked about their work with think-alouds. His answers show a reader less self-aware than Anne, which is just as we would expect of a six-year-old compared to a ten-year-old.

FIGURE 5.15

SELF-ASSESSMENT OF THINK-ALOUDS

Name _Brian_   Date _June_

Teacher _Sue_

1. Here's how I feel about making think-alouds:

   I think it's fun.

2. The best part about my think-alouds is when I

   get pictures in my head and laugh.

3. The part about my think-alouds that I want to change is

   I don't know — maybe read all the words myself.

Figure 5.16 shows a self-assessment for Michele, a ninth-grader. Although she completed this alone, later she was encouraged to share it with a peer group. Michele's insight into what she wants to change in her reading helped other group members talk about their own reading-thinking behaviors. Their discussion about who "owns" meaning was especially thought-provoking for these high school students.

FIGURE 5.16

SELF-ASSESSMENT OF THINK-ALOUDS

Name *Michele*   Date *February*

Teacher *Diane*

1. Here's how I feel about making think-alouds:

They sometimes help

2. The best part about my think-alouds is when I

figure out ideas for things I don't understand.

3. The part about my think-alouds that I want to change is

Having my own opinions and ideas about the topic. I don't like having to learn the author's ideas always — especially when I disagree, like about what a story means.

Summary

We use information from many sources and many different reading activities to understand our students' reading. Our goal is to observe and document their reading behaviors. We believe that this is best accomplished by gathering information using several frameworks. Think-alouds are one framework for gathering and observing students' comprehension.

Think-alouds focus our attention on the thinking processes that occur during reading. They highlight aspects of comprehension that other assessment strategies do not. Think-alouds open a window on how students understand text. They provide a vehicle for exploring students' affective as well as cognitive responses. From our experiences with this procedure, it is probably the best way for us to peek into students' minds to see how each is processing text.

6 Assessing Comprehension Products

The concept of comprehension is a perplexing one. The process involves understanding ideas, words, and actions. Understandings are influenced by past experiences, perceptions, and emotions.

Imagine one eleven-year-old boy's reactions to the world of comprehension assessment! He's the best soccer player in the class, the heart throb of all of the fourth grade girls, and winner of the science fair. He delves into almost all activities with gusto and vigor—except when it comes to reading fiction. Fiction is written in narrative format, and his preferences are for facts based on activities that he is able to act on. His preference for nonfiction was not a problem until he completed a reading test in second grade. The test results moved him from the first reading group to the third. Whether this is fact or fiction, the child's newly acquired perceptions of the situation were firmly established. Reading tests were harmful!

Many student responses to formal test questions are similar to this young man's. Student hesitations about tests, or misunderstandings about test items, often result in answers that cause us to query, "Where did he get that answer from?" We have worked continuously to modify the traditional approaches for assessing the products of reading comprehension. Our endeavors have resulted in the conclusions that RETELLING and the REQUEST PROCEDURE promote close ties between assessment and instruction. They seem to conform to what might be considered the most natural way to find out what students recall after reading.

What Are Retellings and Why Use Them?

The task of retelling matches the goal of reading—to interact purposefully with all of the ideas in a text. Researchers have demonstrated repeatedly that most students who are successful in school reading activities come from literate environments (Teale, 1978, 1981; Holdaway, 1979). These children are read to regularly, which sets them on a path toward happy literacy experiences (Wells, 1986; Chomsky, 1972; Durkin, 1966).

These same natural "reading-to-children" experiences that provided the warm nurturing feelings about language need to continue through school (Cullinan, 1989; Morrow, 1988; Glazer, 1988). When children are encouraged to retell stories as they did to caregivers in the years before school, the home-like environment is recreated (Glazer & Burke, In press).

As children read, they have a natural need to share the ideas from books. They bubble over with enthusiasm as they talk about stories. One of our children spontaneously begins to share immediately after he reads. No matter what we're doing—talking to our department head or a parent, or writing an administrative report— Kevin commands an audience, usually of one, and most often says, "Listen to me. This story was great!" Most situations are NEVER more important than a child's natural responses to reading. Our teachers and administrators as well, except under extenuating circumstances, stop and listen. This reinforces the importance of reading and recalling stories for both the child who is retelling and for others who are observing the activity.

We have found two forms of retelling important for the creative assessment process: unguided and guided formats. *Unguided* retellings are those where students retell without intervention from teachers, peers, or other listeners. *Guided* retellings involve interventions in the form of prompt questions. These prompts are used when children have a difficult time moving through retellings on their own.

It is important for our readers to know that we believe that ANY PROMPTS ARE INSTRUCTION. They influence a student's current and future responses to reading. With that concept in mind, we advise that unguided formats are preferred when assessment and review of children's immediate comprehension of story is the focus.

How to Get Started with Unguided Retellings

Two kinds of unguided retellings demonstrate students' comprehension of story. We use oral retellings for those children who find it easiest to demonstrate their comprehension by talking. We use written formats for those who prefer to write about what they've read. Discovering which mode permits children to demonstrate comprehension best is your first step. Figures 6.1 and 6.2 illustrate that eight-year-old Rebecca's oral retellings provide more content after reading than her obviously scantily written text.

FIGURE 6.1

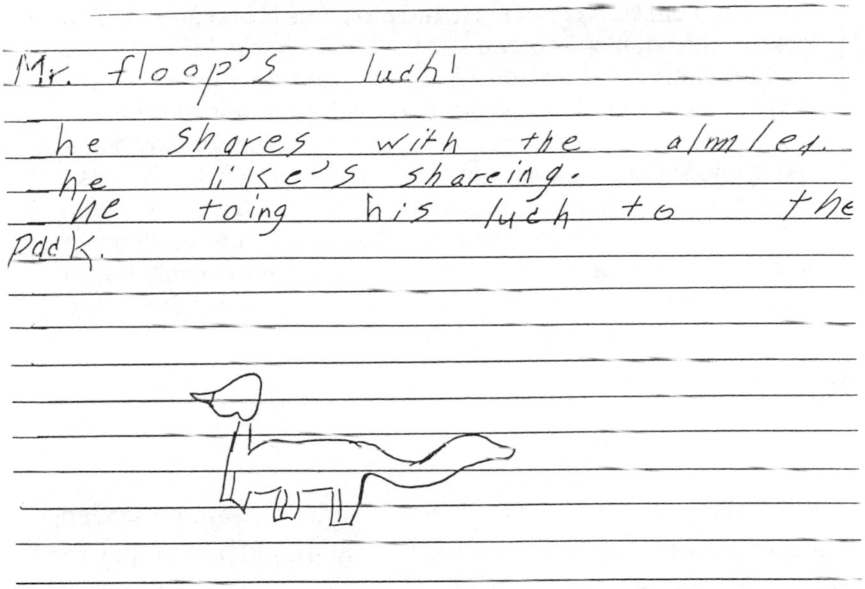

Mr. floop's luch!

he shores with the almlex.
he like's shareing.
he toing his luch to the
Pddk.

FIGURE 6.2

Transcription of oral retelling for Rebecca
Mr. Floop's Lunch by Matt Novak

Mr. Floot's Lunch (whisper...whisper). One day Mr. Floots brang his lunch into the park (whisper...what was the other part). And a... this bird came along and Mr. Floots sat on the seats and he...then more of the birds come and gave it to... and he gave it to them. And then he see.. had no more bread left. Then this dog came along and he gave him sausage and then he gave him his sausage and then all the other dogs came and ate his sausage. Then the squirrel came... then the squirrel came along... then the squirrel came along... (whisper) and um he fed em some (pause) um he fed em some bread. He fed em some bread and then he gave all the other ones bread and then he looked in his lunch bag and he didn't... then he dumped it out and then he didn't see nothing in hus lunch bag and um, and um, he um. And then he was starving to death. And um... then this lady... this old lady came along and she said, "I always come over here to feed the animals." She said... and Mr. Floots came and he said,..."Wait." She said, "This is my favorite bench." She said, "I always come over to bring, to feed the animals some lunch." He said, "I don't think they're hungry and so then she said, "I'll share my lunch with you." And then he said, "I like sharing lunch."

We believe that the best products for demonstrating students' comprehension of story are created IMMEDIATELY after they read that story. In other words, children need to retell, whether oral or written, right after reading their texts. It is also important to select books for retellings that have strong story structures and elements. Students cannot be expected to include elements of stories if the book does not include them.

Fifth-grader Shannon read the short story "Mrs. Gorf" by Louis Sachar. Her retelling is shown in Figure 6.3. Shannon read the story silently and then wrote her retelling. After her teacher reviewed the retelling, using assessment tools mentioned later in this chapter, she discovered several interesting occurrences. Shannon included many of the elements in the story, but those she recalled were from the beginning and the end of the story. Many details, important for indicating that Shannon had understood the story's theme, were omitted.

Teacher's observational notes, which were written on Post-It notes and placed onto the assessment sheet, indicated that Shannon had read rather quickly. She had begun to retell immediately after reading, but never reread her retelling when she completed it. The hastiness, lack of review of her own product, and the content of her retelling seemed to indicate that she read the beginning and ending of the story, but probably skimmed the middle section. Experience with assessing retollings and students' behaviors during these activities helps us to infer these actions.

FIGURE 6.3

One day at schol the first day of schol they got a new teacher the kids said she was the meanest teacher. And the teacher liked apples more then the children, so what she would do is turn the children in to apples. So one morning Mrs. Golf turned 24 children into apples. And there where just 3 more children in there desks. But then when a lady came in she said, Don't you have a lot of apples on your desk. And the teacher said Don't I Well then all of them came back to life. But then the children turned Mrs. Golf into apple. And the children left. Then the Lady came in and

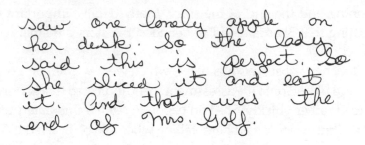

saw one lonely apple on
her desk. So the lady
said this is perfect. So
she sliced it and eat
it. And that was the
end of mrs. Golf.

We are careful, however, when we create inferential statements
such as this about students' behaviors. But we believe that teachers
who spend time with students, interact in an objective manner, use
hard data (products) as well as intuitions to assess and develop
instructional guides are generally on target about students' responses.

Retellings need to be introduced as an assessment tool as part
of the regular school day. We begin the process by using the
following steps.

1. We read or listen to a child read a story to a group of
   listeners.
2. When the reader is finished, our teacher
   IMMEDIATELY retells the story to the group. As she
   retells, using excited stress, pitch, and juncture in her
   voice, she is calling children's attention back to the
   story book and also to the retelling process.
3. After retelling the story, we suggest you say, "Next
   time you read a favorite story, retell it to a friend. Or
   you might prefer to write it in a reading log" (a
   notebook created especially for the collection of
   unguided written retellings, or other responses to
   reading).
4. We hang a wall chart, which includes all of the children's
   names, near the get-together section of the classroom.
   Children, after retelling, sign up to share their written
   retelling with their teacher. Sometimes teachers
   schedule conferences.

5. If the student has retold orally and recorded on cassette tape, the materials must be transcribed. Oral retellings are often transcribed by parent volunteers or teacher aides.
   NOTE: Oral transcripts MUST be written exactly as the students have produced them.

Once our teachers are familiar with assessing retellings and the review process, transcriptions are not always necessary. Listening to the tape can provide the same information about story comprehension.

In addition to our more formal procedures for collecting data, we involve our children in all sorts of retelling experiences. Children read content for research projects, and "retell" the information to peers and adults. After groups walk in the woods, for example, youngsters retell in oral or written format individually or to an audience about their experiences. Observations of the development of eggs-to-chicks, caterpillars-to-butterflies, sand piles-to-ant farm spur children to retell what they've observed. It is important when these spontaneous and planned RETELLING times occur, to notice the points outlined in Figure 6.4.

FIGURE 6.4

Reviewing Retellings

Ideas   Strengths / Needs

Facts are recalled as they

appeared in the text.

Ideas were presented in logical,

sequential order.

Ideas were focused.

Participation was

  —spontaneous---

  —enthusiastic---

  —occurred with prompts---

  —nonexistent---

  —the result of a friend's interactions--

  —the result of a request to respond---

How to Get Started with Guided Retellings

We use guided retellings, as suggested by Morrow (1985), to get children started and guide them to continue when they get "stuck." Morrow (1985), a major researcher in the area of retelling, states that prompting children to retell is instruction. We agree, and with our teachers, insist that classroom assessment procedures replicate instructional practices whenever possible. Prompts, in our estimation, do that, and we've found that we can begin the process with prompts and gradually wean the student away from this dependency.

Like many of our students, you might find that one of your learners sits, turns the recorder on and off, begins and erases, and begins again, and still can't get going. This is the time to intervene. One of our teachers coaxed eight-year-old Jamal to begin by noticing his activities.

Teacher: I see that you've read *Whose Mouse Are You?* I'll turn on the tape (tape is turned on and the teacher talks into the microphone). This is Jamal, and he is going to retell the story *Whose Mouse Are You?* by Robert Kraus. (There is silence, so the teacher prompts Jamal to start by saying "Once upon a time...........")

Jamal: There was a mouse and he was in a cat's house. And---------------------

Teacher: When did the story happen?

Jamal: Um----Um----it happened, uh, in an afternoon. And his, the mouse's family, it was trapped. Yah, the family was trapped.

The teacher noticed that Jamal's eyes were closed during responses. When she asked about this he said, "Oh, I'm making pictures in my mind about the story. I see the mouse and the cat. I see it." Making pictures in one's mind is a useful reader strategy. Retelling in conferences encourages children to retell, and also to inform us about their reading-thinking activities, as well (see Chapter 5). Jamal continued. Each time he stopped, his teacher used a prompt appropriate for eliciting the specific story element needed during that portion of the retelling.

The prompts used, ONLY WHEN NEEDED, for recalling all elements of story are:

When did the story happen? (Setting)
Where did the story happen? (Setting)
Who was the story about? (Main character)
Who were the other characters in the story?(Secondary characters)

What was the problem in the story? (Plot)
What happened first? (Episodic structure)
What happened next? (Episodic structure)
How was the problem solved? (Solution)
What was the theme? (Theme)

It is important to note that children, in most instances, are NOT to look back to the book for information to complete their retellings. If some children have an emotional need to look back, they ought to do this, and a note about this behavior should be included in the observational data.

FIGURE 6.5

Transcription of Oral Retelling for D.J.
Mr. Floop's Lunch by Matt Novak

Mr. Floop packed a lunch one day and went over to the park and he pulled out a roll and a bird came down. He gave a piece of bread and more birds came down and he gave them bread. And then he took out nice juicy sausages and a dog came and he gave the dog a piece of sausage. Then more dogs came and he gave all the dogs the sausages. Then they ran away. The kittens came and he took out poured out some milk and then more kittens came and once all the milk was gone the kittens ran away. And he pulled out peanuts and the squirrel came down a branch and the squirrel... and Mr. Floop gave him a peanut. Be careful not to be getting rabies. He... more and more squirrels came and he gave the squirrel each one of the peanuts for theirselves. When all the squirrels were done they went back into the trees and took a nap. And he pulled out some... oranges and a little... a lady came by and said, "Can I sit down next to you this is my favorite bench. I like to share my lunch with animals." And Mr. Floop said, "They won't be hungry." And she said, "What do you mean?" And Mr. Floop picked up his lunch bag and showed the lady. She smiled and said, "Would you like me to share my lunch with you?" And Mr. Floop said, "A bite or two would be fine." And the lady pulled out a piece of bread and a roll, I mean ... and he said, "I love rolls." The end.

Assessing Retellings

D.J., after listening to his teacher read *Mr. Floop's Lunch* by Matt Novak, carried out an unguided retelling independently. He took his recorder, moved to the library corner, took a pillow and sat with his face turned away from other children to retell. He had often said, "I need to be alone when I retell my stories." Figure 6.5 is the teacher's transcription of D.J.'s unguided retelling.

Figure 6.6 is the teacher's qualitative as well as quantitative assessment of his retelling. The scoring system is one developed by Morrow (1988a). To assess the retelling with the form, check with the student's retelling to notice what elements were included. Be sure that you read the entire retelling before making decisions about inclusion. Give one point for each story element mentioned. Less than one point may be given for characters and episodes. Our older students, children from nine years and up, often quantify their own retellings. We have found that students ready to learn fractions do so easily, for there is a purpose for learning what would normally be a difficult concept. Our students record scores by creating a graph (see Figure 6.12) that provides a visual representation of their achievements.

Qualitative assessment is most important to us. These descriptions provide information about recall of content and also affective responses. Reviewing students' retellings with an "eye" toward the emotional and social reactions to the story as well as the retelling process is ongoing. Notice D.J.'s teacher's comments on the scoring sheet. They include his notion about the possibility of rabies resulting from contact with squirrels. D.J. was able to connect prior knowledge with information from the story. He made the story his own.

FIGURE 6.6

SCORING A RETELLING

Child's Name___D. J._____ Age_____ Grade_____
Title/author of Story_Mr. Floop's Lunch by Matt Novak_ Date_9/15_____
Type of retelling:
        Circle one from each pair: (Guided/Unguided) (Oral) Written; (Listened to/ Read)

Directions: Place "1" next to each element, except as indicated. Partial credit may be given only for characters and episodes (e.g. 4 out of 5 characters equals .8). The highest score for retelling is 10.

SENSE OF STORY STRUCTURE   **COMMENTS**

SETTING:
Begins story with Introduction   1
  Includes time or place   1   _specific reference to park_

CHARACTERS:
Names main character. 1
  Number of other characters named _5_
  Actual number of other characters _5_
  Total score for other characters 1

PROBLEM:
 Refers to main character's goal or problem   1

EPISODES:
  Number of episodes recalled _6_
  Actual number of episodes   _6_
  Total score for episodes. 1   _includes dialogue_
  Proper sequence of episodes. 0

SOLUTION:
  Names problem's resolution. 1
  Ends story. 1

THEME:
  States theme of story. 0

Total score for retelling. . . . . 8 (out of 10)

Affective (personal) involvement with text _D.J. called out reference to "getting rabies" during story's reading. He included this information as part of retelling_
Summary:_D.J. included necessary story elements. Embellished text with reference to squirrels going back to trees to take "a nap." To get started with retelling D.J. needed to sit away from group with teacher close by._
Teacher: _____

Scoring system originated by L. M. Morrow in "Retelling Stories as a Diagnostic Tool," from *Reexamining Reading Diagnosis: New Trends and Procedures*, Susan M. Glazer, Lyndon W. Searfoss, and Lance Gentile (eds.), copyright © 1988 The International Reading Association.

Student Self-monitoring/Assessment of Retellings

Brita's retelling of the same story, shown in Figure 6.7, was written on her own. She, too, set herself apart from other children by standing a large book in front of her desk before she wrote. Brita's teacher completed a retelling scoring sheet, and in addition carried out a self-monitoring conference with Brita. The conference guided Brita to assess her own recall of story. In addition, the conference facilitated Brita's learning of the names of story elements.

FIGURE 6.7

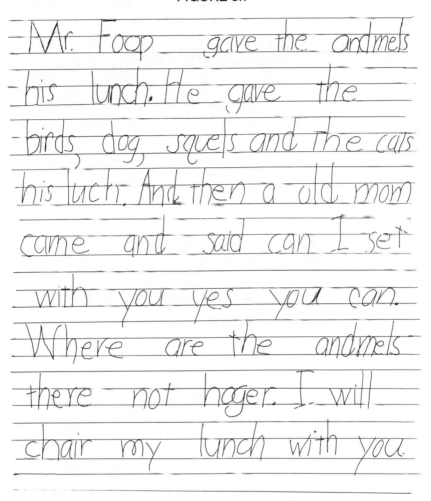

The following dialogue illustrates the procedure used to guide Brita to assess her own work.

Teacher: Hi Brita. Put your retelling here, so we can both see it. Let's read it out loud, together. (Both begin to read. The teacher stops reading with Brita when she is sure that Brita can read through it successfully).

Brita: It was a good story. I liked it a lot.

Teacher: I did too. Now, you and I are going to review your written retelling to see what you remembered. This is a self-monitoring sheet (see Figure 6.8). (The teacher gives Brita a sheet and has another for herself). It includes all of the story elements. (The teacher puts a ruler under the first line) Let's read it together.

Brita &
Teacher: I included an introduction.

Teacher: Brita, find the introduction in your retelling and read it out loud.

Brita: Umm (searching with her finger). Here it is. Mr. Floop gave the animals his lunch.

Teacher: He sure did. And that was how the story began. That's a good way to introduce your story, telling what Mr. Floop did. You could also tell the title.

We move through the self-monitoring tool asking children to justify their responses by locating the element in their text.

Several important factors need mentioning. These include the following:

- When retellings are oral, teachers must read them orally with the child. This is necessary because words in a child's oral language may not yet be part of her reading vocabulary;
- Reviewing retellings by self-monitoring teaches children story structure. Once they internalize the structure by using the tool, they make assessment part of their retelling, and even composing processes. Many of our children have taken the retelling self-monitoring sheet and used it as a guide for creating their own stories.

FIGURE 6.8

STUDENT'S COMPOSITION AND RETELLING CHECKLIST

NAME _Brita_   DATE_____

NAME OF COMPOSITION OR BOOK _Mr. Foop_

AUTHOR _Matt Novak_

	YES	NO
SETTING:		
I began my composition/ retelling with an INTRODUCTION	✓	
I told WHEN the story happened		✓
I told WHERE the story happened		✓
CHARACTERS:		
I told about tho main character	✓	
I told about the other characters	✓	
PROBLEM:		
I told about the story problem or goal	✓	
EPISODES:		
I included episodes	✓	
SOLUTION:		
I told how the problem was solved or the goal was met	✓	
I told how the story ended	✓	
THEME:		
My story has a theme	✓	

When I compose/ retell on my own, I include: _intreduction,_
main character, other characters,
episodes, problem, solution, ending.

The next time I compose/ retell, I need to remember to include these things:_____
where and when the story
happens, more details about the story.

Our teachers regularly record observations of all activities on our three-column progress report sheet. Figure 6.9 was completed by Brita's teacher after her retellings. The review includes Brita's strengths and needs, and plans for future instruction. This sheet serves as a reporting tool, as well as a planning guide.

FIGURE 6.9

PROGRESS REPORT

Student's Name __Brita_____   Teacher's Name __Pat A._____

Time period: From: __Sept._____   To: __Nov._____

AREA: (check one) Comprehension __✓__   Composition____   Vocabulary____
                  Independence/Self-Esteem____   Self-Monitoring____

STRENGTHS	NEEDS (Questions)	PLANS
Brita completed an unguided written retelling of a text, Mr Floop's Lunch, which was read aloud to her in a small group setting. She was able to recall necessary story elements I ncluded dialogue for characters.	Did Brita's giggling during the reading aloud of the story and her preoccupation with the illustrations effect her recall? Would Brita have composed a more complete retelling if she had retold in an oral mode? Would Brita have composed a more complete retelling if she had read the story independently? Did the group setting interfer with Brita's attention to the text?	Conference with Brita using the Student Composition and Retelling Checklist. Discuss the use of picture clues. I ntroduce the fist-full-of-words strategy to help Brita self-select literature to read independently. Have Brita complete an oral unguided retelling.

What is ReQuest and Why Use It?

ReQuest is a procedure which "requests" that students read and develop their own questions about text. Originally developed for instruction by Manzo (1968) and extended by Raphael (1982), the procedure, when modified, is useful for our assessment purposes.

We know that good readers ask questions spontaneously of them-selves and the text in order to clarify understandings (Smith, 1978). Looking at the kinds of questions readers ask about texts as they read provides information about their comprehension.

How To Get Started Using ReQuest

Our major purpose is to determine what information students remember from content reading, such as social studies and science materials, as well as from literature. We are interested in learning about retention of content, and also the student's abilities to infer ideas from the information. Questions written by students provide that information for us.

Our procedure for having students create questions is simple. The process of writing questions fits easily into daily work plans. When our students are involved in a research project, we ask them to read a short section of their content materials. We say, "After you finish the paragraph, or page, or section, write questions about the passage. Write at least two questions."

In a conference, students are asked to test out their questions on the teacher. The goal is for the teacher to answer the questions by finding the information in the text. Once the teacher answers the question, she and the student categorize the question based on the information it seeks. Questions are identified as "right-there," "think-and-search," and "on-your-own" (Raphael, 1982). *"Right-there"* questions are those whose answers can be read "right-there" from the text. *"Think-and-search"* questions ask students to think about the information sought, and then search for the answers. Because answers appear in several places within the body of the text, students must read and search for answers "right-there", and "there," and even a third "there" in the text. "On-my-own" questions are those whose answers are not in the text, but are conceived in the student's mind and are related in some way to the text.

Once we collect students' questions, we review them to notice patterns. We want to discover the types of questions asked. Once we categorize the questions, we are able to determine the kinds of information that each student attends to. Then we redirect our efforts toward teaching them how to write different kinds of questions, which should guide them to attend to different information in the text.

The following passage from a social studies text was used by one middle grade student in one of our classrooms. Questions written by this twelve-year-old in response to reading follow the passage.

New States or a New Nation?

Independence had created not one nation but thirteen. At the time of the Declaration of Independence, when John Adams spoke of "my country" he meant Massachusetts Bay, and Thomas Jefferson meant Virginia. The resolution which announced independence on July 2, 1776, has proclaimed "That these United Colonies are, and of the right ought to be, free and independent States." The first heading at the top of the Declaration of Independence called it "The unanimous Declaration of the thirteen united States of America." They used a small "u" for united because it was still only a hope. (Boornstein & Boorman, 1987, p. 25)

How many nations did independence create?
What did John Adams mean when he spoke of "my country?"
What did Thomas Jefferson mean when he spoke of "my country?"
When did they announce independence?
Whey did they use a small "u" for united?

The teacher and the student noticed, in their conference, that answers to all of the questions could be found by reading them "right-there" in the passage. Instruction was planned for guiding the student to attend to other kinds of information.

Once our students are familiar with the three types of questions, we can flip-flop to instruction and use ReQuest in group settings. Here the group and the teacher (or a student acting as a teacher) read the same portion of text. Then the students write questions and ask them of the teacher, who answers them without looking back at the text. Next they all read another portion of text. Now the teacher constructs questions and asks them of the students. The group discusses the types of question being asked as they are answering them. This activity gives our students practice writing and answering "right-there," "think-and-search," and "on-your-own" questions.

Reporting Progress

Since our children constantly monitor their growth, minimal reporting is necessary. A letter is written to each student summarizing growth over the reporting period. We also report progress to parents in the parent/child/teacher conference (see Chapter 7). We sometimes use a graph and a summary chart to summarize student retellings. Figures 6.10 and 6.11 illustrate these summaries.

FIGURE 6.10

SUMMARY OF INDIVIDUAL RETELLING

I = included
N = not included
NT = not included in the book

Name __Chris__

Date	Story	Introduction	Setting	Main Character	Other Characters	Problem	Episodes	Sequence	Solution	Ending	Theme	Affective (personal) Involvement	Comments
9/15	Mr. Floop's Lunch Oral Unguided read to student	N	I	I	5/3	N	4/6	N	N	I	N	N	Student includes main character, supporting characters, some episodes, and ending. Setting refers to place. Needs sequence and details for reader to follow story. Must include problem and resolution
10/1	My Little Island Oral Unguided read by student	N	I	I	3/4	N	7/7	N	N	I	N	N	Includes main character, supporting characters, all episodes place and ending. Needs introduction problem (clearly stated), resolution, proper sequence and when the story occurs
10/13	Tub People Written Guided read by student	I	I	I	5/3	I	6/7	N	I	I	N	I	Included introduction, main and supporting characters, problem, resolution, ending and setting. Guided prompts have resulted in student including more elements. Still needs proper sequence and additional details.
10/30	Frosted Glass Written Unguided read by student	I	I	I	5/5	I	8/8	I	I	I	N	I	All necessary story elements included. Provided reader with details in sequence Still needs to identify when story action takes place.

FIGURE 6.11

SUMMARY OF RETELLINGS

Name *Chris*   Time Period: From: *Sept.*

To: *Nov.*

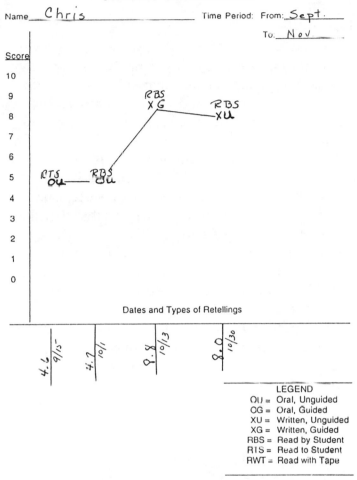

Dates and Types of Retellings

LEGEND
OU = Oral, Unguided
OG = Oral, Guided
XU = Written, Unguided
XG = Written, Guided
RBS = Read by Student
RTS = Read to Student
RWT = Read with Tape

These graphs and summary charts are attached to a letter similar to the following.

Dear Chris,

You and I have decided to review four retellings as evidence of your growth in story comprehension during this reporting period. The information has been written on the summary sheet, and on the graph. You will notice that you increased your comprehension during this time.

When you began retelling in September, you included the place the story happened, called a setting, the name of the main character, and a series of episodes. Your first two retelling scores were lower then than the last two.

After using prompts, you remembered more, and your scores went up. In September I asked you to retell orally. That was a mistake. You prefer to retell by writing about the story.

I am especially happy that you learned to monitor your own comprehension. You even calculated your retelling scores, and charted them on the retelling graph.

Your retellings are like your compositions. You included all of the elements at the beginning. You need to work on including a problem and solution.

We discovered that you wrote "on-my-own" questions almost all of the time. You and I and Jamal, Brita, and Rebecca met several times to learn how to write other types of questions. Now you are learning to make up "right-there" and "think-and-search" questions.

Best wishes,
Your Teacher, Mrs. Abitabilo

Summary

We agree that comprehension is hard to understand and difficult to assess. It is impossible to "look into children's minds" as they read. We have found ways to collect data about the products of their reading, which gives us information about children's ideas as they attempt to make meaning from text. We can never be sure if we are correct about how they think. However, we can tell what they recall, and have obviously processed, by looking at their products—retellings and questions about the books they read. We tried carefully, for the minds of children are individuals who come to school with independent perceptions about themselves as readers and the content they read about. Our procedures attempt to respect the unique qualities of each. We therefore describe success with the intent of helping students to help themselves read more effectively.

7 Reporting Progress: Students, Teachers, and Parents Collaborate

"How'd I do?" "Is my child on grade level?" "Will I make the honor role?" Comparing performance, one student to another, has perpetuated the use of report cards in our country. Our current system is influenced by the first I.Q. test administered in 1917, when the nation was seeking quantitative ways to determine growth. Tests like those that measure I.Q. provide a "one-snapshot" view of performance.

Recent massive changes in instruction are forcing educators to alter assessment and reporting procedures. Classrooms are changing so that many sources and types of work samples are being used to determine growth. Students are beginning to "take charge" of decisions that describe their advances during school time. Teachers are gaining confidence about their professional judgments based on knowledge and experience. Perceptions of growth by those involved in classroom activities are beginning to take center stage, sometimes over results of standarized tests.

Our approach to assessment conforms to current educational practices. The approaches which you've already reviewed are based on teacher, as well as student decisions, opinions, and evaluations of samples of work and the effectiveness of the strategies they use to complete this work. Our process encourages students and teachers to:

1. Ask themselves questions about strengths and needs;
2. Collect and review data (performance samples) with the questions in mind;

3. Collect the data over time (a week, month, or several months); and

4. Answer the questions or restate them to match the data.

The approach is based on the C-A-L-M (a suitable acronym for collaborative notions about growth) approach to assessment (Glazer & Searfoss, 1988). We acCumulate data, to Assess Language growth over time. Figure 7.1 illustrates the framework around which our alternative assessment procedures are based. The C-A-L-M approach supports our notion that multiple tools, multiple environments, and multiple strategies for collecting and sorting data are essential for describing students' performance. It provides a model for reviewing students' growth, and also a framework for teachers to observe their effectiveness as facilitators of language learning.

FIGURE 7.1

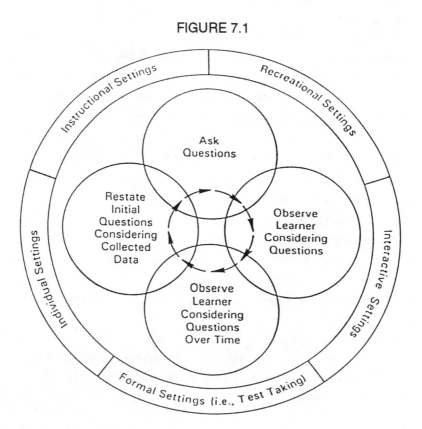

You have reviewed daily, weekly, and summary reports. This final chapter includes procedures that we hope you will use to replace the traditional report card system used throughout the school year.

Collaborative Reporting Procedures

The daily and weekly assessment procedures included throughout this text are the basis for sharing accomplishments with parents several times during the school year. Parents are invited to a conference where the child shares accomplishments. The following letter is one way to introduce parents to the new procedures. We mail this home after one month of school each fall.

> Dear Parent(s),
> Welcome to the new school year. Our staff spent many hours this summer working on an alternative to our report card system.
> Three conferences will be scheduled, one each in November, March, and May. (student's name) will attend the conference with you. He/she will share his/her accomplishments for each reporting period during this time. This new procedure is designed so that (student's name) knows what he/she has learned, and what he/she needs to work on. Our staff feels that it is important for children and parents, together, to learn about activities in school.
> If you have questions, do call me during school hours. I would be happy to chat in person, as well.
>
> To a good school year,
>
> Gary Turner
> Principal

Preparing for Conferences

Routine reviews prepare students to discuss and share their retellings, compositions, and other work samples. We find that when we pass children working, we stop when the time is appropriate and ask that they tell us about what they are doing and what they've learned. They thumb through their collections of data and respond, by pointing to examples. Many youngsters volunteer to share regularly. More formal reviews with the teacher are scheduled, in addition to retelling and other conferences, at least once a month. Children's enthusiasm for these meetings is illustrated by Jon's note to his teacher. It read:

FIGURE 7.2

Dear Mrs. Poole,
        Don't forget we have a meeting. It is Tuesday at 2:15. I will tell you every thing I learned.

Love,
Jon

Unlike retelling conferences which extend for not more than ten minutes, final conferences can run between twenty and forty minutes. Preparation for these individual conferences includes:

1. Regular reviews of data collections;
2. Making the checklist a "natural" part of daily activities;
3. Engaging students in developing the format for the parent/child/teacher conference.

We mail a letter to parents two to three weeks prior to the scheduled conference date. We send a reminder home with the child one week before conference time. A sample follows.

Dear Parent,

The end of our assessment period is two weeks away. We are scheduling child/teacher/parent conferences for (date). You, (student's name), and I will meet to share accomplishments and goals. (student's name) and I hope that all of us leave the conference with similar perceptions of (student's name) strengths and needs.

Please call the school office to confirm our appointment. I look foward to meeting with you and (student's name) on (date).

Sincerely,

(teacher's name)

The Parent/Child/Teacher Conference

Warm greetings, and an explanation of the session can be carried out by the child, himself/or herself. The teacher might assume this role, if the child prefers. Each should have a copy of the conference checksheet. Figure 7.3 is the checklist completed by Jon during his conference.

FIGURE 7.3

CONFERENCE GUIDE

Student's Name: *Jonathan*   Date: From: 2/5/92
Teacher: *Barbra pool*   To: 4/10/92

SOME THINGS I LEARNED	COMMENTS

WORK HABITS

I use a contract to organize my work.
yes I did

I ask for help when I need it.
yes sometimes

I pay attention.
yes when I like wat I am dowing

I need my teacher to help me pay attention.
No

I pick my own books to read.
yes

I use the "fist-full-of-words" to pick books. *Yoy put ror fist up and your fingers up if you dowt know a word*

I talk, out loud, to myself to remember things.
No

I talk to friends about my work.
yes

ABOUT MY WRITING

My favorite topic to write about is:
The simsins

Sometimes I "brainstorm" before I write.
sometimes

Sometimes I use a map to write a first draft.
Sometimes

I get ideas for writing from books.
yes spyete spgete

I get ideas for writing by talking to my teacher or a friend.
yes

After I write my first draft, I reread it.
Sometimes

Sometimes I ask a friend to read it.
No

I can edit some of my writing by myself.
I put in ponits

I write in my journal each time.
yes

I keep a reading log.
yes

ABOUT MY READING COMPREHENSION	COMMENTS

I like to read about:
The simsins

I remember what I read when I read out loud.
yes I rememben

I remember what I read when I read to myself.
sometims

Pointing helps me keep my place when I read.
So I No wat I am

I show what I remember after I read, by retelling out loud.
No

I show what I remember after I read by writing a retelling.
yes

I can self-monitor my retellings.
by looking at my reading log.

I know "right-there" questions.
yes

I know "think-and-search" questions.
No

I know "on-my-own" questions.
we didint do them

HOW I LEARN NEW WORDS

I guess what a word s when I read.

yes

I learn words by saying them and tracing them.

yes

THINGS I DO, THAT GOOD READERS DO

Before I read, I look, think, and then predict.

yes

I reread when I don't understand.

yes

I make a picture in my mind.

No

I predict what comes next.

yes

I make believe that I am a character in the story.

No

I ask myself questions.

No Yes

OTHER THINGS THAT I LEARNED

writing about storys

THINGS I'D LIKE TO CHANGE

Working

The dialogue below answers questions about procedures.

Teacher: (directing talk to parents) Jon and I have prepared to share our accomplishments over the past three months (or school year). The copy of the checklist in front of you includes all of the strategies that are part of our integrated language arts curriculum.

Jon: And all of my work samples are in this basket. I have folders in here too with work in them. (Looks at his teacher) Should I start?

Teacher: Sure!

Jon: I am going to read each thing on the list. You can look at yours when I read it (Jon points to their copy). Mrs. Freidman has one (points to the checklist) too. She is going to read it to herself when I read it. Then I am going to

write my answer in the space. And Mrs.
Freidman is going to write her answer in the
space.

Parent: What if the answers are different?
(The teacher and Jon look at each other. Jon
proceeds to answer.)

Jon: It doesn't matter. If I can tell "why" I wrote
the answer, it's O.K. There is no wrong answer.

Teacher: Ready Jon?

Jon: Uh, huh.

Parent: Where are you starting?

Jon: Up here, Mom (pointing to the first item).

Teacher: O.K., Jon. Let's read the first item together.
(The teacher and Jon read the first item together, as if in a chorus. This choral reading
proceeds for three items. When the teacher is
confident that Jon is able to read it by himself, she discontinues reading with him.)

At times during conferences our teachers ask children to
demonstrate strategies they've learned. Youngsters will also use
their baskets of work samples to justify accomplishments. Many
often select one of their products and talk about it. The discussions
range from reading the content to describing the processes which
were involved in creating each sample. Jon, for example, enjoyed
demonstrating his ability to edit his stories. He also derived great
pleasure from describing how he selected books by using the fist-
full-of-words rule. "You just hold all your fingers up. Then you read,
and when you make a mistake a finger goes down. When they're all
down, guess what? The book's too hard. Then you pick a different
one."

At the end of these conferences, all participants feel part of the
learning situation, and have learned, together, what has been accomplished in school.

Final Yearly Report

A written report follows each conference. We write this report in the form of a letter to the student. The letters usually include the following:

- Goals for the student;
- Strategies used that guided the student to accomplish these goals;
- Recommendations for the future; and
- Books read.

Letters are an extension of daily, weekly, and monthly review activities. We have made the decision to include ONLY positive results of instruction and to report what is not learned as "needs." The positive nature of the language in the letters serves to build the intrinsic motivation for literacy learning that we strive for. You may want to use the letter format for all areas of the curriculum.

> Dear Jon,
> I can't believe that the school year is ending. I have enjoyed working with you.

> Composition

> You and I developed the following goals for this reporting period. These goals are an extension of those we've set during this school year. Our goals included:

> 1. To get better at including a problem and a solution to that problem when writing stories;
> 2. To get better at refining a draft for publication;
> 3. To refine self-monitoring skills for (1) composing and (2) editing;
> 4. To get better at using writing to share your ideas with others;
> 5. To learn new words from memory to use in your writing.

> You've learned to prompt yourself in order to remember to include a problem in your stories by saying to yourself,

"Did I include a problem in my story?" I hear you do that when you are working by yourself. You are including problems in almost all of the stories you write. Sometimes you write the solution to the problem first, and then you write the problem in the margin where it belongs. You did that in your story about *The Zurangle From Planet Platinum*. You told how the Zurangle got back to Planet Platinum before you included that Zurangle got lost.

You also reread your final draft and recorded it on tape. This helps you put in punctuation. You asked for editing help from me, sometimes, too.

Jon, you wrote five short stories, and one long one. Your long story was like a chapter book.

You also learned to write 100 words from memory since March. Wow!

I have found lots of letters in my mailbox from you. You also wrote in your journal everyday. We have shared lots of things about ourselves. I hope that you continue to write during the summer.

The Comprehension Process

1. To work on noticing when you don't understand when you're reading;
2. Making pictures in your mind to help you understand new vocabulary.

You seem to enjoy using think-alouds to help you understand what you read on your own. This is new for you. You have learned to say, "I don't understand that word." Then you think about what you need to do to help yourself understand the text. You have told me that you close your eyes, and try to picture what is happening in a book, and that helps you to understand what you read better. I do that sometimes, too. This is a great strategy.

When you are reading this summer, try to predict what will happen next. Read and ask yourself, "Am I right?" Predicting during reading is also a good think-aloud to use on your own. I hope you continue to think about your reading, at home, this summer.

Comprehension Products

1. To continue to self-monitor your retellings, and include more details;
2. To remember to state the main goal or problem and resolution after reading stories;
3. To retell in creative (alternate) ways.

You have learned how to monitor your own written retellings. You don't even need me to help you get started. I was so excited to see your comments about your retellings. Once you wrote, "I forgot the problem just like in my own story."

You read 20 books in Ed Packard's *Choose Your Own Adventure Series* since September. You recorded each book on your "Books I Read" sheet. Each time you finished one you said to me, "Mrs. Freidman, I finished another one!" You also read other adventure stories. Adventure stories seem to be your favorite.

You might like to keep a log this summer, and write down things you want to remember after you read. You know, Jon, writing about things you and your family do is like retelling. You might want to keep a diary.

Independence

1. To manage your own work schedule;
2. To ask for help from your teacher, when you need it.

Jon, you are an independent worker. It makes me feel good to watch you use your contract. You complete one activity. Then you sometimes write a summary of what you did. Then you look at your contract, and begin to work on the next task. You have developed wonderful work habits that will help you all the way through school.

Jon, A final message for you

I have enjoyed you as a student. You are also a fun person to be around. You smile a lot, you listen to others when they need to talk, and you know when to talk, yourself. You have a special way of deciding to do something. You stick to the task until it is done. I have watched you work with other students. You are a good helper.

Sometimes you get a bit impatient. I think that's because you need to learn that each of your friends is different from you. That means that each one learns a little faster or a little slower then you do.

You have a very special trait. You are willing to try new things. Sometimes you even do things that I am hesitant to do myself. Do you remember the time we went on the field trip to the planetarium? The doors were locked. The whole class just stood in the rain, waiting. You went up to the security guard and asked if we could go in. That did it. We got in. I think that's terrific.

I hope that you have a good summer and great vacation.

Love
Mrs. Belanger

Summary

Reporting is a continuous process. It evolves in our classrooms as an interactive, productive, cooperative endeavor between peers and teachers. When assessment becomes a natural part of the school day, assessment becomes instruction. Exchanging ideas regularly in collegial settings facilitates an inner drive to learn.

8 Questions Teachers Ask

Susan: I just came back from conducting a three-day inservice with 88 teachers in Montana. Then I went to New York State, and discovered that no matter where I work with teachers several questions arise again and again.

Carol: I've had similar experiences. Inservice teachers as well as our graduate students all seem to worry about many of the same things concerning alternative assessment.

Susan: For the sake of our readers, Carol, let's list questions and then dialogue in order to satisfy all of our readers.

About Organizing

Question 1.   This system sounds great! But how do you manage to find time for all of this?

Susan: Most teachers are concerned with managing time so that they can work individually with children.

Carol: Managing time for conferencing with individual students means setting up a flexible schedule. Many teachers set aside a two to three hour time block in the mornings. They begin at 9:00 and work on language arts activities until 11:30.

Susan: Some children work collaboratively on projects during the time block. Others work on their own. Children read and retell during this time, carry out writing activities, and think-alouds as well. A conference schedule is created by the teacher and posted. Children and teachers schedule individual conferences for reviewing retellings and compositions. Of course, all children are not scheduled daily. Our teachers see approximately five children each day. Decisions about who is to have a conference are made jointly.

Carol: Some teachers schedule children who are most in need of individual attention. We have found that an individual conference every ten days is a good target. Conferences that last five to fifteen minutes provide more individual instruction then forty minute group activities.

Question 2.   How do I get started?

Susan: We found that scheduling one morning or afternoon weekly is a good way to begin. Children look foward to the unique organizational plan. Our teachers talk about the changes with the children. It is amazing how many good ideas children from ages 6 to 16 come up with. Many make their own time management plan.

Carol: What you've really addressed, Susan, is how to get started with an integrated language arts program.

Susan: You're right. But I have a difficult time separating alternative assessment from the instructional program because of the flip-flop nature of realistic assessment in classrooms, or in life itself, for that matter.

Question 3.   Is it really possible to save all of children's work?

Carol: Sure, if you want to.

Susan: I think teachers mean how do you manage all of the paper. It can be cumbersome with 30 children.

Carol: We've discussed storing or categorizing students' work samples in Chapter 3, which we called "Frameworks For Getting Started." What we've found is that classrooms have different ways of storing things. We've also learned that kids develop their own way of storing things. Some children have a big box which they use as a personal file In other classrooms, children share file drawers where they keep folders of work. Some teachers like to start with in/out baskets like the kind that are used in offices. In some rooms work gets saved in categories, like "math," "writing," "science." In others, it all gets saved together.

Susan: I've found that children and teachers often come up with unique ways of storing samples. One child, for example, stored stories that she had written at the beginning of the school year in a tube that is usually used to mail posters. She had it marked, "My September and October Writing."

Question 4.   But when do you stop saving and start sorting out?

Carol: When the containers get full, or at regular intervals that the teacher or children set up, or as the children themselves decide they need to organize. What's important is that the work samples get sorted regularly, so that those samples that are saved represent growth over time. Students don't need to save everything indefinitely, just long enough so they can see their work in a particular area over a period of time.

Susan: For example, Jon saved every single piece of writing for about a month. Then he decided he had too much. So he scheduled himself for a conference with his teacher, Miss Carroll. When they met, she asked him, "What do you want to save, Jon?" Jon's shrug indicated that he needed more guidance. "Well," his teacher continued, "You may want to save the things that will show your mom and dad, at the conference, how you've learned to rewrite drafts." Without further direction, the nine-year-old pulled out his first draft, his third, and fourth, which was the final draft for the story he had written. "I don't need to save the second one," he commented. "I didn't do anything very different in that one."

Carol: I'm suggesting that Jon and other children save multiple drafts of only a few pieces of writing during a reporting period, not everything. Choices need to be made periodically, based on what children and teachers want to report to parents and other professionals. Childrens' choices must also be considered. It's important to consult with the student about what to show. Then they need to attach assessments to those work samples.

About Composing

Susan: You know, Carol, most of the teachers I've worked with ask few questions about the composing process.

Carol: That's probably because they've been doing a great job of teaching the writing processes.

Susan: You're probably right. Questions dealing with composing usually focus on the mechanics of writing, and audience awareness. These follow.

Question 5.   *When are invented spellings*
inappropriate?

Carol: Children develop naturally in their ability to represent
sounds that they hear with written symbols. They progress
through predictable stages of development. We can't
rush their growth by stopping them from using invented
spellings. Once we analyze their spelling patterns,
however, then we can decide what to help them learn next
about how our language works. For example, if they are
representing words with beginning and ending
consonants, then we help them to represent the vowel
sounds they hear in the middle of the words as well.

Susan: The purpose for the writing can help us decide whether or
not to help a student use correct spelling. If a student is
writing a draft, we are interested in their ideas and in how
they organize them. We want them to be fluent. If the
writing is for sharing, what we call publication, then we
help students spell correctly. We have a three-step process.
Students read through their compositions themselves to
see if there are spelling errors. They put a circle around
each. If they can spell the word correctly, they write the
word on top of the circle. If they can't, they make a list and
ask peer editors of their teachers for help.

Question 6.   *What do you mean by audience*
awareness?

Susan: James Moffett is probably responsible for coining the
term. He used it to discuss the distance between a text and
the reader. Some texts are written, explained Moffett, for
oneself and, therefore, an audience consists of only the
writer. At the other end of the spectrum is public writing.
That's writing for an audience of thousands, most of
whom the writer does not know. So when we look at a
student's writing and ask, "How aware is the student of

her audience?" we are in a sense asking, "Is he writing for personal or public consumption?" The more public the piece, the more formal and mechanically correct it must be.

About Comprehension Processes

Carol: Think-alouds are new to many teachers.

Susan: I think they're new to most. I've not been in a school district yet where more than about three percent have heard of them, at the most.

Carol: Questions usually focus on an explanation of the processes involved in making think-alouds. Many of these questions are answered in Chapter 5, but other questions also get asked.

> *Question 7.   How are retellings and think-alouds different?*

Carol: Students retell after they have finished reading a book. They think aloud while they are in the process of reading. One is a product of the reading, the other is an in-process activity. One relies on memory, the other on moment-by-moment thinking.

> *Question 8.   Should a teacher pronounce a word for a child when he is in the middle of making a think-aloud?*

Susan: That depends on the purpose for the activity. If the teacher wants to assess the student's thinking behaviors while reading, then probably not. Seeing how the student thinks when he or she does not understand a word, for example, can help guide instruction.

Carol: Well sometimes it's useful to pronounce the word for the student so he can continue to think about the meaning of the text, especially if it's a young reader. Students can also think aloud about a text that is read to them. Then they listen and think aloud.

> **Question 9.**   *Does it matter whether the student or the teacher chooses the text for a think-aloud?*

Susan: Our students like to choose the texts, although sometimes we ask them to think-aloud with texts we select. They feel more in control when they choose the text, and this usually helps them think about the text more easily and confidently. This confidence is important, especially during assessment activities.

> **Question 10.**   *When students stop to think aloud, don't they interrupt their comprehension?*

Carol: We hope that what they are doing is comprehending out loud, not stopping their comprehension. We know that when students makes a think-aloud they must stop their reading and think about the text. This slows down their reading, but the process is almost an instructional one for some students. They learn that slowing down and thinking more helps them comprehend. This, eventually, helps them to help themselves comprehend independently.

Susan: Do you mean that students learn how to think more clearly about what they're reading?

Carol: That's exactly right! What they also learn is that thinking takes a long time. So they learn how to slow down and think, and slowing down is O.K. The notion that "faster is better" gets abandoned.

About Comprehension Products

Susan: Most of the questions that I'm asked about the products of comprehension deal with scoring retellings. Before answering them I'd just like to emphasize that SCORES ARE NOT AS IMPORTANT AS RECOGNIZING WHAT IS RECALLED. We've continued to use scores because they provide a means to create a visual picture of growth. They also provide a real reason for children to learn fractions. Questions, however, follow.

> *Question 11.   How do you score a retelling if a theme, in the retelling, is implied rather then stated.*

Carol: Scoring is personal and subjective. Sometimes teachers give students a point for an implied theme. Other times they don't. It's interesting—children are usually harder on themselves then their teachers. Often teachers score retellings higher then children.

Susan: Theme is really a difficult concept to understand, especially for young children. Often they do, in fact, infer what the theme actually is. But they have a difficult time expressing the ideas specifically. This is when instruction takes over. If you assess their ability to identify the theme is a problem, use prompts to guide youngsters.

Question 12   *Is it important that children remember episodes in the right order?*

Carol: Now that's a good question! Think about how many things you can remember after you read a story. I can recall most of the story, but I find it difficult, at times, to remember all of the episodes, especially if there are seven or more. We're not too concerned about the order in which the children remember the episodes, unless the order affects the story's theme or outcome.

Susan: Carol, I've found that teachers are also concerned about how to determine how many episodes there are in a book, especially chapter books.

Carol: This is really a thorny question. I don't think it's important. What is important is that students remember the episodes that affect the theme and outcome of the story. Older students often summarize many episodes in retellings. Younger children tend to retell using every detail they can remember. Teachers have to use their common sense. They have to be readers themselves, join reading groups, and talk about real books they're reading. And they need to notice how they respond themselves when they retell.

Question 13.   *What if a story doesn't have a theme?*

Carol: Then it's probably not a good story to use for retelling purposes. Stories used to review children's growth in comprehension must have definitive story structure. In other words, they have to be well written, and include all the elements of story. If they are not, we are not fair to the child, or the assessment process.

Question 14.   *What if a child does a retelling, and you KNOW that he or she didn't read the book?*

Susan: Great question! That happens a lot at the beginning of each of our lab sessions. Some of the kids retell without reading. When we have a retelling conference and use the self-monitoring sheet, it all comes out right in the end. When children review their retellings, we ask them to justify the content by referring back to their text. When justification is not possible, then our teachers ask the child to find the answer in the text. One youngster, after moving through this process, said to his teacher Janet, "I think I made up the answer because I forgot what the book said."

Carol: So, once children discover that they must read the book, because the assessment process DEMANDS it, retelling without reading stops.

Susan: The procedure itself is self-monitoring.

Question 15.   *Some children retell best orally, and don't like to write. Should all children, at one time, retell in writing?*

Carol: Lots of teachers ask this question. Retelling is done so that children have a product that results from reading. The product, the retelling, provides information about what each child recalls. Some children retell best by writing and others demonstrate comprehension best orally. Every child must use his or her best mode, written or oral, to demonstrate retelling.

Question 16. *What do you do when you are working*
with one child, and another interupts?

Susan: Another great question, Carol. Each of our teachers creates a signal. When Kaye works with a child, she puts on her "do not disturb cap." That means, don't talk to either of us until we are finished with our conference.

Carol: Sometimes I hold up a finger, and never even look at the child, and that works. Some of our teachers touch the child who is attempting to interrupt gently on the shoulder.

Susan: Most important is letting children know that interruptions cannot happen, except when there is an emergency. Interruptions cause distractions. This does not help the student or the teacher stay on task.

Reporting Progress

Susan: Of all of the questions, those that deal with reporting progress seem most cumbersome.

Carol: I have a problem with them as well. Teachers seem especially concerned about how to tell parents, children, and school administrators what children have learned.

Question 17. *Do you ever use standarized tests?*

Susan: Important question! Yes we do. The emphasis placed on the results, however, is quite different then it is for most. We look at a test score as just another small piece of data. We continuously remind ourselves that the score is similar to a snap-shot or photo. It makes a picture of the moment.

Carol: What we look for is patterns in performance across different kinds of work samples and tests. We have been successful in convincing our population of children and parents that tests are no more important than the work samples, our observations, and their observations and perceptions of progress.

Question 18.   What about report cards?

Susan: Teachers ask us that question all the time. Our answer is consistent. The reporting systems need to match the assessment procedures. If they do not, then inconsistency causes confusions. If we record descriptively, then reporting must also be descriptive.

Carol: And if quantitative measures—test scores—are the basis for determining growth, then grades or scores on report cards may be appropriate.

Question 19   How do we convince administrators that this is going to work?

Susan: We decided that this question was a good one to close with.

Carol: I agree. Now let's see. The best way to convince administrators that alternative assessment procedures work is to just do them. Once principals and superintendents see demonstrations of growth, you will win them over.

Susan: The most exciting thing for me is to watch the children self-monitor their own growth. I suggest that your school administrator be invited into your classroom. Ask a child to volunteer, and have her review self-monitoring procedures and results with the administrator. You might

ask the child to share your letter to her—the one written
at the completion of a reporting period—as well.
What better evidence of growth then a child telling,
"What I know and what I need to work on!"

Epilogue

Twelve years have led us to the contents of this book. We continuously change procedures to meet the needs of our student population. We attend many conferences and read many professional journals and books as well. We talk to each other frequently, monitoring the development of materials. Most importantly, our personal interactions with children and colleagues help us think about what "works" with students. The continuous nature of our self-monitoring guides us to make our classrooms healthier and more successful places for us all.

Although our assessment and instructional procedures will CONTINUE to change, our goals are consistently the same. We strive to create independent teachers and learners who:

- take risks;
- take responsibilty for their learning;
- make decisions about how and what they learn; and
- feel in control when using the language arts to learn.

References

Adams, M. J. (1991). *Beginning to read: Thinking and learning about print.* Cambridge, MA: MIT Press.

Adams, M. J., Grundine, H., & Morrow, L. M. (1992, May). In J. Manning (Chair), *Decoding Emphasis and Literature Based Reading Programs: Are They Incompatible Curriculum Views?* Symposium conducted at the meeting of the International Reading Association, Orlando, FL.

Afflerbach, P., & Johnston, P. (1984). Research methodology on the use of verbal reports in reading research. *Journal of Reading Behavior, 16*(2), 307-322.

Ashton-Warner, S. (1963). *Teacher.* New York: Simon & Schuster.

Atwell, N. (1987). *In the middle: Writing, reading, and learning with adolescents.* Portsmouth, NH: Boynton/Cook-Heinemann.

Bereiter, C., & Bird, M. (1985). Use of thinking aloud in identification and teaching of reading comprehension strategies. *Cognition and Instruction, 2*(2), 131-156.

Bertrand, J. E. (1991). Student assessment and evaluation. In B. Harp (Ed.), *Assessment & evaluation in whole language programs* (pp. 17-33). Norwood, MA: Christopher-Gordon.

Bond, G. L., & Dykstra, R. (1967). The cooperative research program in first-grade reading instruction. *Reading Research Quarterly, 2,* 5-142.

Brown, A. (1980). Metacognitive development and reading. In R. J. Spiro, B. C. Bruce, & W. F. Brewer (Eds.), *Theoretical issues in reading comprehension.* Hillsdale, NJ: Erlbaum.

Brown, C. S. (1988). Merging assessment and instruction: Protocols in the classroom. In S. M. Glazer, L. W. Searfoss, & L. Gentile, (Eds.), *Reexamining Reading diagnosis: New trends and procedures* (pp. 94-102). Newark, DE: International Reading Association.

Brown, C. S. (1988). Think Aloud: A method for teaching the processes of comprehension. *The Reading Instruction Journal, 32*(1), 13-17.

Burke, E. M. (1990). *Literature for young children* (2nd ed.). Boston: Allyn & Bacon.

Butler, J. (1980). Remedial writers: The teacher's job as corrector of papers. *College Composition and Communication, 31,* 270-277.

Calkins, L. M. (1986). *The art of teaching writing.* Portsmouth, NH: Heinemann.

Campbell, C.A. (Chair) (1992). *The National Education Goals Report 1992.* Washington, DC: U.S. Government Printing Office.

Chall, J. (1967). *Learning to read: The great debate.* New York: McGraw-Hill.

Chomsky, C. (1972). Stages in language development and reading. *Harvard Educational Review, 42,* 1-33.

Clark, H. H., & Clark, E. V. (1977). *Psychology and language.* New York: Harcourt Brace Jovanovich.

Clay, M. (1975). *What did I write?* Portsmouth, NH: Heinemann.

Clay, M. (1983). Getting a theory of writing. In B. M. Kroll & G. Wells (Eds.), *Explorations in a development of writing.* New York: John Wiley & Sons.

Clay, M. (1991). *Becoming literate: The construction of inner control.* Portsmouth, NH: Heinemann.

Collins, A., Brown, J., & Larkin, K. (1980). Inference in text understanding. In R. J. Spiro, B. C. Bruce, & W. F. Brewer (Eds.), *Theoretical issues in reading comprehension* (pp. 385-407). Hillsdale, NJ: Erlbaum.

Cullinan, B. E. (1989). *Literature and the child* (2nd ed.). San Diego: Harcourt Brace Jovanovich.

Davey, B. (1983). Think aloud—modeling the cognitive processes of reading comprehension. *Journal of Reading, 44-47.*

Durkin, D. (1966). *Children who read early.* New York: Teachers College Press.

Ericsson, K., & Simon, H. (1980). Verbal report as data. *Psychological Review, 87*(3), 215-251.

Farr, R. (1992). Putting it all together: Solving the reading assessment puzzle. *The Reading Teacher, 46* (1), 26-37.

Glazer, S. M. (1991, August/September). Resoling an old shoe. *Teaching, K-8,* 121-124.

Glazer, S. M. (1992). *Reading comprehension: Self-monitoring strategies* to develop independent readers. New York: Scholastic Professional Books.

Glazer, S. M. (1992, May). Assessment in classrooms: Reality and fantasy. *Teaching, K-8, 62-64.*

Glazer, S. M., & Burke, E. M. (In press). *A developmental approach to literacy: From literature to language.* Boston: Allyn & Bacon.

Glazer, S. M., & Searfoss, L. W. (1988). *Reading diagnosis and instruction: A C-A-L-M approach.* Englewood Cliffs, NJ: Prentice-Hall.

Glazer, S. M. & Searfoss, L. W. (1989). Reexamining reading diagnosis. In S. M. Glazer, L. W. Searfoss, & L. Gentile (Eds.), *Reexamining reading diagnosis: New trends and procedures* (pp. 1-11). Newark, DE: International Reading Association.

Glazer, S. M., Searfoss, L. W., & Gentile, L. (Eds.). (1988). *Reexamining reading diagnosis: New trends and procedures.* Newark, DE: International Reading Association.

Goodman, K. S. (1986). *What is whole about whole language?* Portsmouth, NH: Heinemann.

Goodman, K. S., Smith, F. B., Meredith, R., & Goodman, Y. M. (1987). *Language and thinking in school: A whole-language curriculum* (3rd ed.). New York: Richard C. Owen.

Goodman, Y.M. (1989). Roots of the whole language movement. *The Elementary School Journal, 90(2),* 113-127.

Graves, D. H. (1983). *Writing: Teachers and children at work.* Portsmouth, NH: Heinemann.

Hahn, J. (1981). Students reactions to teachers' written comments. *National Writing Project Network Newsletter, 4,* 7-10.

Haley-James, S. (1982). Helping students learn through writing. *Language Arts, 59,* 726-731.

Halliday, M. A. K. (1975). *Learning how to mean.* London: Edward Arnold.

Harste, J. C., Burke, C. L., & Woodward, V. A. (1982). Children's language and world: Initial encounters with print. In J. A. Langer & M. T. Smith-Burke (Eds.), *Reader meets author/bridging the gap.* Newark, DE: International Reading Association.

Holdaway, D. (1979). *The foundations of literacy.* Sydney: Ashton Scholastics.

Hosenfeld, C. (1979). Cindy: A learner in today's foreign language classroom. In W. Borne (Ed.), *The foreign language learner in today's classroom environment.* (pp.53-75). Montpelier, VT: Northeast Conference on the Teaching of Foreign Languages.

Huey, E. (1908). *The psychology and pedagogy of reading.* New York: Macmillan.

Hynds, S. (1989). Bringing life to literature and literature to life: Social constructs and contexts of four adolescent readers. *Research in the Teaching of English, 23*(1), 30-61.

Kintgen, E. (1985). Studying the perception of poetry. In C. Cooper (Ed.), *Researching response to literature* (pp.128-150). Norwood, NJ: Ablex.

Kroll, B. M. (1978). Developing a sense of audience. *Language Arts, 55,* 828-831.

Loban, W. (1976). *Language development: Kindergarten through grade 12.* Urbana, IL: National Council of Teachers of English.

Loughlin, C. E., & Martin, M. D. (1987). *Supporting literacy: Developing effective learning environments.* New York: Teachers College, Columbia University.

Manzo, A. V. (1968). *Improving reading comprehension through reciprocal questioning.* Unpublished doctoral dissertation, Syracuse University.

Michaels, W. & Karnes, M. R. (1950). *Measuring educational achievement.* New York: McGraw-Hill.

Morrow, L. M. (1985). Retelling stories: A strategy for improving young children's comprehension, concept of story structure, and oral language complexity. *Elementary School Journal, 75,* 647-661.

Morrow, L. M. (1988a). Retelling stories as a diagnostic tool. In S. M. Glazer, L. W. Searfoss, & L. Gentile (Eds.), *Reexamining reading diagnosis.* Newark, DE: International Reading Association.

Morrow, L. M. (1988b). Young children's responses to one-to-one story readings in school settings. *Reading Research Quarterly, 23,* 89-107.

Morrow, L. M. (1989). *Literacy development in the early years: Helping children read and write.* Englewood Cliffs, NJ: Prentice-Hall.

Neuman, S. B., & Roskos, K. (1992). Literacy objects as cultural tools: Effects on children's literacy behaviors in play. *Reading Research Quarterly, 27,* 203-225.

Newman, S. (Ed.). (1985). *Whole language theory and use.* Portsmouth, NH: Heinemann.

Olson, D. (1977). From utterance to text: The bias of language in speech and writing. *Harvard Educational Review, 47,* 257-281.

Olson, G., Mack, R., & Duffy, S. (1981). Cognitive aspects of genre. *Poetics, 10,* 283-315.

Palincsar, A. S., & Brown, A. L. (1984). Reciprocal teaching of comprehension-fostering and comprehension-monitoring activities. *Cognition and Instruction, 1*(2), 117-175.

Petty, W. T. & Finn, P. J. (1981). Classroom teachers reports on teaching written composition. In S. Haley-James (Ed.), *Perspectives on writing in grades 1-8* (pp. 19-34). Urbana, IL: National Council of Teachers of English.

Piaget, J. (1967). The genetic approach to the psychology of thought. In J. P. DeCecco (Ed.), *The psychology of language, thought and instruction.* New York: Holt, Rinehart & Winston.

Raphael, T. E. (1982, March). *Improving question-answering performance through instruction* (Reading Education Report No. 32). Urbana: University of Illinois, Center for the Study of Reading.

Rasinski, T. V. (1989). Reading and the empowerment of parents. *The Reading Teacher, 43,* 226-231.

Routman, R. (1988). *Transitions: From literature to literacy.* Portsmouth, NH: Heinemann.

Ruddell, R. B., & Haggard, M. R. (1985). Oral and written language acquisition and the reading process. In H. Singer & R. B. Ruddell (Eds.), *Theoretical models and processes of reading* (3rd ed.) (pp. 63-80). Newark, DE: International Reading Association.

Rummelhart, D. (1977). Toward an interactive model of reading. In S. Doric (Ed.), *Attention and performance VI.* London: Academic Press.

Russavage, P. M., & Arick, K. L. (1988). Think along: A strategic approach to improving comprehension. *Reading: Issues and Practices, 5,* 32-41.

Searfoss, L. W., & Enz, B. J. (1991). *The integrated/holistic classroom observation and assessment guide.* Tempe, AZ: Reading Library Science, Arizona State University.

Searfoss, L. W., & Readence, J. E. (1989). *Helping children learn to read* (2nd ed.). Englewood Cliffs, NJ: Prentice-Hall.

Searle, D., & Dillon, D. (1980). The message of marking: Teacher written responses to student writing at intermediate grade levels. *Research in the Teaching of English, 14*(3), 233-242.

Smith, F. (1978). *Understanding reading* (2nd ed.). New York: Holt, Rinehart & Winston.

Smith, N. B. (1965). *American reading instruction.* Newark, DE: International Reading Association.

Sommers, N. (1982). Responding to student writing. *College Composition and Communication, 33*, 148-156.

Sperling, M., & Freedman, S. (1987). A good girl writes like a good girl: Written response and clues to the teaching/learning process. *Written Communication, 4*, 343-369.

Stein, N. L., & Glenn, C. G. (1979). An analysis of story comprehension in elementary school children. In R.O. Freedle (Ed.), *New directions in discourse processing II* (pp. 53-120). Norwood, NJ: Ablex.

Teale, W. H. (1978). Positive environments for learning to read: What studies of early readers tell us. *Language Arts, 55*, 922-932.

Teale, W. H. (1981). Parents responding to their children: What we know and need to know. *Language Arts, 58*, 902-911.

Teale, W. H. (1990). The promise and challenge of informal assessment in early literacy. In L. M. Morrow & J. K. Smith (Eds.), *Assessment for instruction in early literacy* (pp. 45-61). Englewood Cliffs, NJ: Prentice-Hall.

Temple, C. A., Nathan, R. G., & Burris, N. A. (1982). *The beginnings of writing.* Boston: Allyn & Bacon.

Valencia, S. W., & Pearson, P.D. (1987). Reading assessment: Time for a change. *The Reading Teacher, 40*, 726-732.

Valencia, S. W., Pearson, P. D., Peters, C. W., & Wixson, K. K. (1989). Theory and practice in statewide reading assessment: Closing the gap. *Educational Leadership*, April, 57-63.

Vygotsky, L. S. (1962). *Thought and language* (p.101). Cambridge, MA: MIT Press.

Watson, D. J. (1989). Defining and describing whole language. *The Elementary School Journal, 9(2)*, 129-146.

Wells, G. (1986). *The meaning makers.* Portsmouth, NH: Heinemann.

Whisler, N., & Williams, J. (1991). *Literature and cooperative learning: Pathway to literacy.* Sacramento, CA: Literature Co-op, 2020 7th Avenue, 95818.

Wilson, R., & Russavage, P. M. (1989). Schoolwide applications of comprehension strategies. In J. D. Coley & S. S. Clewell (Eds.), *Reading issues and practices* (pp. 45-46). Maryland: State of Maryland Reading Association.

Children's Literature
Mentioned in This Text

Avi (1991). *The man who was Poe.* New York: Avon Books

Boornstein, D. & Boorman, R. (1987). *The landmark history of the American people (Vol. 1) from Plymouth to Appomattox.* New York: Random House.

Eastman, P.D. (1966). *Are you my mother?* New York: Random House.

George, J.C. (1972). *Julie of the wolves.* New York: Harper & Row.

How things work (1982). Chicago: World Book-Childcraft.

Kellogg, S. (1977). *The mysterious tadpole.* New York: Dial Press.

King, D. & Anderson, C. (1980). *America: Past and present.* Boston: Houghton Mifflin

Kraus, R. (1972). *Whose mouse are you?* New York: Macmillan.

Mayer, M. (1968). *There's a nightmare in my closet.* New York: Dial Press.

Novak, M. (1990). *Mr. Floop's lunch.* New York: Orchard.

Packard, E. (1979). *Choose your own adventure,* a series. New York: Bantam.

Sachar, L. (1980). Mrs. Gorf. In H. Weiss & J. Weiss (Eds.), *More tales out of school* (pp. 30-34). New York: Bantam.

The Authors

Susan Mandel Glazer is Professor of Education at Rider College, Lawrenceville, New Jersey, where she is Coordinator of the Graduate Program in Reading/ Language Arts and Director of the Center for Reading and Writing, both of which she founded in 1980. She received her Ed.D. from the University of Pennsylvania. She is author and coauthor of numerous articles and books. Dr. Glazer will serve as President of the International Reading Association in 1994-1995.

Carol Smullen Brown is Assistant Professor of Education at Rider College, where she teaches graduate and undergraduate courses in Reading and Language Arts. She is Chair of the Undergraduate Education Department.

Phyllis DiMartino Fantauzzo is Assistant Director of the Reading and Language Arts Clinic at Rider College, as well as a School Psychologist and Reading Specialist. She received both her Master of Arts and School Psychologist Certification from Rider College.

Denise Healy Nugent received her Master of Arts from Rider College, where she is an adjunct instructor in graduate education as well as reading clinician at the Reading and Language Arts Clinic.

Lyndon W. Searfoss is Professor of Education at Arizona State University. He is an author or coauthor of numerous articles and books, including *Helping Children Learn to Read, Second Edition* and *Reading Diagnosis and Instruction: A C-A-L-M Approach*, with Susan Mandel Glazer.

Index

Self-monitoring, 38–41
  behaviors, 38–39, 74
  conferences, 40, 65, 72
  tools, 65, 67–68
Self-Monitoring Retelling Sheet, 76, 80
Sketches, classroom, 11
Spelling development, 62
  invented spellings, 62
  reviewing spellings, 62
  rules, 62
  Spelling Trend Analysis Sheet, 62
  trends, 62
Story structures, 54–55, 59, 60
Strengths, summary of, 35
Students' performance samples, work samples, 162
Students' self-assessment of learning; self-monitoring tools, 22

"Task force" (colleagues, visual arts specialists, school administrators, and so on, 32
Teacher
  narratives about students, 34–35
  notes, 34–35
Teacher's observational notes, 119
  wall chart, 120
Test scores, 1–2, 3–4, 162
  standardized, 2, 4, 7, 9
Text, appearance of, 47
Think-alouds, 12, 13, 34, 37, 87–114, 152
  advantages, 88, 89
  to assess comprehension, 89, 114, 156–158
  assessing, 94–95
  directions, 88–89, 90, 92–94
  how to get started, 90

process, 87–88, 92–93, 114, 156–158
samples, 95–106
selecting text, 90–91, 95
settings, 93
student interest, prior knowledge, 101, 125
Think aloud work, self-assessment of, 103, 105, 110–112

Whole language, 7–8
  holistic learning, 8
Writing
  beginning stage, 51, 52, 58
  definition of, 47, 48
  developmental process, 47, 48, 84
  elements of, audience awareness, 155 156
  instruction, 51
  kinds of, 54
    narrative, discourse, 54 55
  mechanics of, 47, 48, 154
    capitalization, 47, 50
    neatness, 47
    punctuation, 47, 50, 52
    segmentation, 47
    spelling, 47, 50, 155
  stages, 47
Writing Assessment Summary Sheet, 50, 51, 54
  audience awareness, 51
  mechanics, 51
  sentence construction, 51
  writing stage, 51, 52
Writing samples, 34, 35, 37, 38, 54
Writing Stage Assessment Sheet, 51
  complete thoughts, 51
  sentence
    patterns, 52
    starter(s), 52